CLASSIC
COUNTRY HOUSE
HOTELS

CLASSIC
COUNTRY HOUSE
HOTELS

— CAROL WRIGHT —

Photographs by Eric Crichton

PAVILION
MICHAEL JOSEPH

First published in Great Britain in 1989 by
Pavilion Books Limited
196 Shaftesbury Avenue, London WC2H 8JL
in association with Michael Joseph Limited
27 Wrights Lane, Kensington, London W8 5TZ

Designed by Andrew Barron Associates
Photography by Eric Crichton
Cartography by Ken Vine

A CIP record of this book is
available from the British Library

ISBN 1-85145-317-2
Library of Congress Catalog Card Number 88-91457

10 9 8 7 6 5 4 3 2 1

Printed and bound in Spain by
Graficas Estella

The photograph on page 3 is of Tanyard in Kent

CONTENTS

INTRODUCTION

The Gilt Back on the Gingerbread

Noël Coward, a frequent visitor to Hambleton Hall, described in this book, summed up the plight of 'the Stately Homes of England' in his witty song for *"Operette"* as long ago as 1938; they were a financial headache, then as now:

Tho' the fact they have to be rebuilt
And frequently mortgag'd to the hilt
Is inclin'd to take the gilt
Off the gingerbread . . .
The Stately Homes of England
We proudly represent,
We only keep them up for
Americans to rent . . .

The Second World War did not do much to help the larger manor house. Many became schools, military hospitals and institutions of various kinds. After the war, a few optimistic souls battled with rationing and coupons to open hotels in such houses. Sharrow Bay in the Lakes and Greywalls in Scotland were pioneers. Later, Martin Skan at Chewton Glen strove for perfection both in hotel and restaurant, evolving a standard that he still seeks to improve upon. In the sixties and seventies cheap charter sun flights and pricey British hotels made staying at home seem less attractive to Britons, but the Americans appreciated the history, antiques and off-beat welcome of manor house hotels which the British are only now discovering as superb bolt-holes within easy reach.

Now, in the eighties, the country house hotel is the fashionable place to go for weekends in the country, top-level board meetings and shooting parties – even if the target is only clays. The world of Wodehouse has returned; the clack of croquet mallets is heard the length and breadth of the land, and indoors the click of cue on ball as old billiard rooms are reopened.

Some country house hotels even have the stately butler to greet guests, and maids in

Old brick and beams give a mellow background to the fresh dining ideas at Whitehall.

Decoration of one sort or another is typical of the country house hotel.

Victorian frilled pinafores to turn down beds, pop in a hot water bottle and tidy away clothes. Above all it is the individual decoration and style of the rooms that appeals; a reaction against the nightly filing boxes of international hotel chains; the same twin beds, a table cum desk that is not suitably lit or designed for either task, the luggage rack that is too narrow, the standard lobby bathroom and closet with theft-proof hangers, and notices of do's and don'ts and sales literature on every surface.

Henry James, who travelled extensively and stayed at many hotels in England, sums up the current appeal of the country house hotels. 'Of all the things the British have invented . . . the most perfect, the most characteristic . . . is the well appointed, well administered, well filled country house.' Country roads are now over-hung with many signs to 'country house hotels', though not all live up to the subtle definition and parameter which have governed the selection of hotels for this book. Converting houses into hotels is certainly one way of preserving Britain's rich heritage of country houses of all sizes and styles, and buying and running a country house hotel seems now as popular as retiring to a country pub was a few years ago. Some families have bought spacious houses to provide a more splendid home setting for themselves and support this by acting as hoteliers.

The style of country house hotels is as varied as their architecture and owners. My definition of the true country house hotel is that, when you arrive, the host, his wife or their dog greets you, and you then sign a visitor's book (or, as at Cliveden, a bedroom guest book) not a form, on a side table, not a reception desk. The rooms, like the guests, should be named, not numbered. Some country house hotels don't even provide keys; at some you have to ring the bell for admittance as at a friend's house, and some put guests' names on little white cards on their doors. Mini bars are horrid anywhere and especially so in country houses, though they do exist. Tea makers are often provided, but more usually a request for tea or coffee brings a well-set tray with linen cloth, strainers, varied kinds of sugar, a cafe-tiere for coffee, and a plate of home-made cookies; often on fine china with family silver pots and utensils. Many places welcome with sherry or other drink and fruit bowl in the room, while the biscuit barrel of goodies by the bedside pioneered by Sharrow Bay has become a country house hotel trademark less crass than the chocolate on the pillow of larger hotels. Cliveden supplies a whole tray of decanters of spirits, mixers and sherry for each guest.

A formal bar exists in many of these hotels but is not of the essence of a country house hotel, which should have a drinks tray or table in a sitting room or discreet dispense bar. Cromlix has its bottles arranged in a Victorian invalid chair to wheel around the drawing room.

The small size of many country house hotels and the need to have a good chef leads many owners to insist on a dinner/bed and breakfast tariff, particularly in the Lakes and northern England, and often a set menu served at a set time. But the table is yours for the whole evening, and after the meal there are often enough separate sitting rooms for each group to have a quiet cup of coffee served by an open log fire.

Open fires, flowers from the garden, even laundry baskets of home-made pot-pourri or dried flowers (as at Congham Hall) scent the rooms decorated with antiques and plenty of personal possessions; china, books and glossy magazines, cats and dogs and even caged birds are all part of the household. Many country house hotels do accept pets to stay or have kennelling in the grounds, though some hosts make enquiries about the character of canine visitors for the sake of their own pets. Rooms are frequently given homely touches: Wood Hall and Stapleford Park offer house teddy bears as comforters, and Egerton Grey has a cradle full of dolls and soft toys, belonging to the daughter of the house, for guests to borrow.

The relationship with the host should be a more personal one, though he may impose some house rules; after all, the house is his home too. Hosts will advise on local sights and things to do and often provide the means to do them. Stocks of wellies, anoraks and sports gear in the hall are a happy sign. There is the story of the American who told his country house hotel host he wished he had more time in England as he would have liked to find a good gun dog to take home. Next morning at breakfast he found a puppy tied to his chair leg. It was explained that this was a gun dog of high pedigree. 'Put it on my bill,' said the satisfied guest.

In its ample grounds the country house hotel will usually provide sports facilities, of the sort associated with country houses, such as croquet, tennis, riding, fishing, shooting or clay pigeon shooting. Congham has its own cricket ground, some houses have golf courses, and several have helicopter pads for the smart business lunch party.

Though fire doors have to be installed, and other alterations may have to be made in original structures to comply with regulations,

Topiary at Billesley Manor, Warwickshire.

ideally the country house should not be extended much beyond its original size. One can
forgive the away-in-a-manger offering of converted stables, coach-houses, dovecots, cottages and follies or barns around the house.
There are excellent examples – Bodysgallen
and Middlethorpe – of how this can be done
sympathetically, and Lucknam has made fine
use of its courtyard coach-houses as a health
club. But jarring modern spur wings have often
been added for conference facilities, to make
the project more 'viable', diluting the essential
country house party atmosphere. The more
caring owners make sure that non-conference
guests are not swamped; some insist that the
whole house is taken for the holding of meetings; and taking the whole dozen or so rooms is
a happy idea for a wedding party or special
private occasion, or a winter sporting weekend.

The country house hotels selected for this
book are a subjective collection of places as
near to the ideal as possible, but embracing
every kind of architectural style and historic age
from castles to cottages, from manors to
medieval farms; sometimes sleeping in history
compensates for shortcomings of decor.

Some of my selections date back to the
Domesday Book, others to the Tudor period;
there are stately Georgian blocks, Victorian
industrialist's gentrification status symbols and
homes built in the Edwardian era, the heyday of
the house party. Some were built as splendid
family homes even for kings and princes, some
as shooting lodges and holiday homes; others
were working farms and humbler dwellings;
one is a cottage. In mid Wales there is even a
Victorian workhouse (not in this book) that calls
itself a country house hotel. But to qualify for
inclusion in this book all had to have been
originally built as private dwellings in country
settings.

Against each property I have indicated
'proprietor' or 'owner' and the names. There is
not much of a distinction in meaning between
the two words, but 'proprietor' has the addi-
tional connotation of 'whether in possession or
not', so I have used this word to indicate a chain
ownership, however small, or an absentee
landlord; while 'owner' is used to show where
the owner is resident and runs the property,
though in some cases resident owners have the
assistance of professional managers, and where
these play a particularly important role in the
relationship with guests I have put in their
names as well. Owners who have worked hard
through the season are more likely to take off
in winter to recoup strength, or to use this
period to catch up on household maintenance,
so it is important to check opening dates

which are likely to vary from year to year.

The ideal host is the owner with his family, one member of which perhaps being chef. But chains are now realizing that the one-off historic house with professional managers in charge can become a flagship for their company, and there are one or two companies now specializing in country house hotels. Even the National Trust is turning hotelier with a property like Cliveden in Berkshire which is featured in this book. For ease of reservation those country house hotels belonging to marketing consortia such as Relais, Prestige, Pride of Britain and Wolsey Lodges (for smaller private houses) have a note to this effect alongside them and addresses of these organizations are found at the end of the book.

The country house hotel can also be a source of ideas for interior decoration: many use the latest designer fabrics very effectively, draping them over four-posters, half-testers and canopied beds, and around windows of every size and shape. Birgitte Skan at Chewton Glen and Ruth Watson at Hintlesham Hall are ladies to watch for decoration ideas, and Glenborrodale Castle is a place to see how china plates can be hung on walls to great effect. Stapleford Park shows off more flamboyant ideas, and Egerton Grey makes unusual use of antiques; old bagatelle tables are used for coffee service.

The gardener will also delight in many country house hotels admiring and examining

Detail from a ceiling painting in the morning room at Pale Hall, Gwynedd.

the plants and trees. Several Victorian houses have the arboretum collection of specimen trees beloved of that time. Many country house hotels have gardens which have been restored, in accordance with their original designs, as carefully as the house; there is a seventeenth-century Dutch knot garden at Bodysgallen; a huge herb garden at the Elms at Abberley, and 1¼ acres of formal herbs at Grafton Manor; important walled kitchen gardens at Hope End and Glenborrodale; formal parterres at Cliveden; and Hartwell House has gardens laid out by a pupil of Capability Brown. The Manoir aux Quat' Saisons has lovely water gardens, and vegetable gardens with unusual French vegetable varieties; Congham Hall has recreated an old-fashioned potager, and the gardens at Gravetye are a memorial to William Robinson, the great nineteenth-century gardener and tree expert. Gertrude Jekyll got her inspiration from more cottagey settings, and her designs can be seen at Little Thakeham and Greywalls. Some hotels sell their garden plants or generously give away cuttings, as at Congham. Greywalls offers 'garden interest breaks'.

Many country house hotels not only use their gardens to grow their own fruit, vegetables and herbs, sometimes even rearing their own chickens and goats (as at Hope End), but have access to local game, fish and farm produce. They have also done Britain the greatest service in showing the world that Britons can cook superbly. The scattering of *Michelin* stars and other guide commendations among country house hotels reflects the number of excellent, mostly young chefs working far from the bright city lights and forging their own recipe reputations. It was always said the best British food was found in private houses – and country house hotels have continued that tradition, right from the early days of Francis Coulson at Sharrow Bay, with his wonderful English menus, and John Tovey at Miller Howe; while Neil Bannister at Tullich Lodge showed that the set menu did not have to mean the end of the diner's right to choose but could be a balanced bill of fare that educated the palate and gave impetus to new flavour ideas. In some hotels, *cordon bleu* cooks prepare the menus or the lady of the house cooks her favourite dishes.

While chefs like Shaun Hill at Gidleigh Park forge ahead with new and eclectic recipe ideas, many are researching and recreating traditional recipes, particularly puddings: bread and butter, Queen of puddings, treacle sponge and even the humble and long forgotten (at least by caterers) blancmange and jelly. Cromlix has its family collection of game recipes; Cliveden is

Sundials and croquet epitomise the leisurely pace of life in country house hotels.

researching old English puddings, and the housekeeper's book of the Astors' heyday there shows that the French influence on cooking was a hallmark of upper-class country house eating, a tradition followed by young country house hotel chefs who use French classical expertise with local produce. Raymond Blanc, described by many as Britain's leading chef, made his name independently of both France and London, and his manor house restaurant with its produce gardens is the perfect setting in which to enjoy his creations. Country house hotels have indeed extended the frontiers of the good life, both in bedroom comfort and style, and in flavoursome food. The country house owner always kept a good cellar and his hotel descendant does too; the list seems to lengthen in inverse proportion to the size of the restaurant and lists embrace wines from all round the world; one hotel, Thornbury Castle, has its own vineyard and sells its own label wine.

Country house hotels are not always the cheapest of accommodation, but they give visitors the enchantment of sampling a lifestyle and setting of the past; waking to a tea tray brought by a maid, with fine china, flowers and newspaper; looking out on parkland, trees and gardens; eating fresh produce; reading to one's heart's content on big window seats, day beds or on chintzy sofas by the fire, not crushed or pressurized by crowds; being looked after, even cosseted; and after sports or walks, going back to a hot bath in an old claw-footed tub before dinner – perhaps with ducks to play with or a toy yacht as at Flitwick Manor.

A gargoyle at Oakley Court surveys the former setting for horror films.

| **A+** over £150 | **A** £100-£150 |
| **B** £70-£100 | **C** under £70 |

As prices inevitably escalate, I have arranged the cost in a graded system as above though rates should always be checked out. The price is usually per double room; when dinner and full breakfast are included, as indicated, the prices become much more of a bargain.

The details of ownership, chefs and facilities were correct at the time of going to press but this is a volatile business: chefs move, owners sell or move on, chains acquire other properties, and newcomers continually appear. Stately family homes that dodge becoming a school, nursing home or company HQ are now back in the business of hospitality, that their original owners dispensed so freely, and country house hotels are a booming trend in tourism, taking people out from the cities and providing something unique and essentially British for everyone to enjoy.

CAPITAL COUNTRY

The Great Wen of London has spread mightily since Dr Johnson gave it that epithet. Where once nobles and gentry built their country retreats, there is now encircling suburbia. But the buildings and their peaceful gardens remain, making easily gained bolt-holes and, for visitors to the capital, a more relaxing venue for stays than the city centre hotel blocks. Other country house hotels are close to London's airports, making them useful stop-over havens. With judicious use of motorways, deeper country retreats can be reached quickly, and all the following are within an hour's drive of the capital.

Starting with one of the grandest and most stately of country house hotels, Cliveden, the former home of the Astor family and richly decorated with architectural 'souvenirs' from Jacob Astor's travels, is set in 375 acres of estate on a bluff above the Thames. It was first built in 1666 by the Duke of Buckingham, a favourite of Charles II; its owners have included several dukes, as well as Frederick Prince of Wales, and it was the Duke of Westminster who sold it to the Astors. The portrait of Nancy Astor by Sarjeant hangs in the huge hall. It was she who willed the estate to the National Trust on condition that some public access was maintained. The National Trust now maintains the fabric of the house and gardens, and the public are admitted to the grounds and, on certain afternoons on time tickets, to some of the public rooms. Although the hotel is quite separate from this, guests may occasionally find themselves the subject of fascinated stares as they take their afternoon tea by the vast fireplace brought from a French château in the main hall.

Cliveden opened as a hotel in March 1986 after £3 million had been spent on restoration, offering 25 rooms named after owners of the house or famous guests. The only single, 'Rudyard Kipling', has a curious wall bed. The 'Duke of Buckingham' is dark panelled with contemporary portraits and prints of the house. 'Mountbatten', in the old billiard room, still has the scoreboard on the wall. 'Sutherland' has a portrait of Charles I over the pillared stone fireplace. The 'Prince of Wales' suite on the upper floor is in pale blue silk with views over the formal parterres. Nancy Astor's bedroom, popular with honeymooners, has white-painted panels, huge portraits, rose chintz drapes and quilts, and a carved Italian fireplace. It also has the only terrace.

Each room has its own guest book, so you can find out just who has been sleeping in 'your' bed. The gas 'log' fires are lit before each guest

One of several carved figures guarding the staircase at Cliveden.

Previous pages: Gravetye Manor near East Grinstead, West Sussex.

Cliveden
Taplow, Berkshire SL6 0JF
☎ (06286) 68561
Proprietor: The National Trust. Member of Prestige
Director and General Manager: the Hon. John Sinclair.
Price grid A+

Location: Leave M4 at Exit 7, slip road for half a mile, to roundabout, left onto A4 towards Maidenhead; after half a mile roundabout, turn right at roundabout towards Burnham; four miles to T-junction opposite Cliveden main gates; in grounds follow 'house guests' signs.
45 minutes central London. Helicopter pad (2 hours notice). By rail to Maidenhead or Taplow; car collection can be arranged. By boat; own moorings at Cliveden Reach.

arrives, and with low, almost candle-power lighting an atmosphere of the past is produced, not always easy on the eye when trying to read up on the Cliveden art collection, reclining on a day bed and sipping a drink from the complimentary side table of crystal decanters, bottle of sherry and mixers.

There used to be five bathrooms in this house where guests were the rich and famous of the day, but many have now been added in former dressing rooms with old-style claw-footed tubs, dressing tables, and wardrobe areas – any clothes left out will be folded and put away by the maid. A light breakfast including chocolate-filled croissants can be served in the rooms on a well set tray, the newspapers looking as if they have been ironed. Downstairs a full Edwardian buffet spread is set out in the French dining room, with its panelling from Madame de Pompadour's château and the original long dining table. The dining room, the former Astor drawing room, faces the garden and is shaded by champagne-coloured blinds. Chef Ron Maxfield from Portsmouth offers a wide range of dishes, from elegant salmon and caviar parcels to rabbit with garlic mustard sauce, but is keen to expand a repetoire of traditional British recipes.

Nancy Astor's Wedgwood blue boudoir, the Tote room, Great Hall and library are among the rooms in which you can take coffee and read newspapers. Outside, the huge estate is now worked by nine gardeners, as opposed to the fifty of the Astors' time. Wellies will be brought on request by a butler, and swimwear is also loaned. Squash and billiards are indoor pastimes, and there is an exercise room with sauna

The formal parterres in Cliveden's grounds.

and steam area. Across the courtyard below the ornate clock tower is the walled swimming pool, heated in summer, which became notorious in the Profumo scandal. The estate offers tennis, croquet, riding, good walking, as well as fishing on Cliveden's own stretch of the Thames. A walk at Cliveden can take in the tree under which prime minister Canning wrote his speeches, summer-houses and little temples, the fountain of love, formal gardens with clipped hedges, water gardens where a two-week open-air festival of Shakespeare is held in June/July, and the amphitheatre where 'Rule Britannia' was first performed.

While Cliveden headlined in media scandals, Oakley Court was the setting for other kinds of drama. You may have seen its Charles Addams-effect turrets, windows and gargoyles before. The derelict house was used by Hammer Horror films as the setting for Dracula's castle, with candles used to light the entire house; as well as in *Murder by Death*, the *Rocky Horror Show* and happier films like *Half a Sixpence*.

The 35-acre gardens with large monkey puzzle trees lead down to the Thames with croquet, a nine-hole pitch and putt course and private coarse fishing. The hotel can arrange boat trips and can charter Cliveden's *Suzy Ann*, a restored Edwardian river launch. Oakley Court was built in 1859 by Sir Richard Hall-Saye for his French wife and styled as a Gothic château. Guarded by gargoyles with forked tails and huge jaws, the public rooms include the drawing room where afternoon tea is served, the library (Alastair Sim's study in *St Trinians'*)

Oakley Court was once used as Dracula's Castle for a film.

Oakley Court
Windsor Road, Water Oakley, Windsor, Berkshire SL4 5UR
☎ (0628) 74141
Proprietor: Norfolk Capital Hotels. Member of Prestige
Price grid B

Location: Leave M4 at Exit 6 towards Windsor; A308 towards Maidenhead; Oakley Court is 3 miles on the right. There is valet parking: a tag is attached to your car keys to show where the car has been put.
Own Heliport. By rail Waterloo to Maidenhead or Windsor.

and a billiard room with open fire and gothic roof light and a 300-year-old table. Of the 9 rooms in the main house eight are named after previous owners. The landing was once a minstrels' gallery, and the current owners are considering whether to reinstate it.

General de Gaulle was a regular visitor during the Second World War, and Oakley Court was said to be the English headquarters of the French resistance. No resistance is needed to succumb to chef Murdo MacSween's menus. A nephew of Sir Compton Mackenzie and formerly at Walton's restaurant, Mac-Sween has ideas varying from daily roasts and traditional steak and kidney comforters to light modern dishes such as poached christophine with smoked haddock and pink peppercorn sauce.

T he proximity to London of thickly wooded countryside and heathlands derives from the former royal passion for hunting. Windsor Great Forest, in which Bagshot is one of few communities, was allowed to exist because James I and Charles I kept a hunting lodge there. Later it became an important coaching stage between London and Salisbury and it was on Pennyhill that highwayman William Davis sought refuge from the king's men. It is a refuge still, the nineteenth-century house standing peacefully in its park of 112 acres.

Though Charles II had a hunting lodge on the site, Pennyhill Park dates from 1849, created by James Hodge, a builder by profession who designed and built the first structure to span the St Lawrence river. The entrance, flagged and flower-bedecked, leads to a sweeping staircase lit by stained-glass windows. On the ground floor, a loggia in blue and white with a Georgian feel is a perfect place for coffee and the morning papers in the morning sun overlooking the terraced gardens to parkland beyond and the hotel's own trout lake. Nearby is the Pennyhill Park Country Club, for which hotel guests have membership and where light meals and saunas can be taken. There are tennis courts, riding, a golf course and clay pigeon shooting, with professional tuition provided for the shooting, riding and golf.

The beamed Elizabethan-style Latymer restaurant is the setting for roast-off-the-trolley executive lunches and where seasonal produce is served with updating touches such as Scottish salmon with warm wholemeal brioche; caramelized duck breast is braised with Sauternes and fanned on a papaya sauce. Vegetarian menus are available, and the dinner selection includes a vegetarian dish. Local

Pennyhill Park
College Ride, Bagshot, Surrey GU19 5ET
☎ (0276) 71774
Owner/manager: Brian Murphy. Member of Prestige

Location: Off M3 at Exit 3 towards Bagshot, and through village; in the High Street turn left on to A30 and right up Church Road to College Ride. 27 miles from central London.

The Georgian-style sun room is the place for coffee and cats at Pennyhill Park.

venison and pheasant come from the nearby crown estates, and there is an in-house bakery and herb garden.

The old coach-house has been skilfully converted to thirty bedrooms linked to the old house by a redwood arched walk giving a total of 48 rooms each named for a shrub or a flower. In the coach-house there are romantic high-beamed roofs; one bedroom has a cleverly designed open-plan bathroom, with old beams used as a room divider, and the bed has a canopy pleated and flowing up to a cross-beam. In the main house the Hayward suite (named after the last resident owner) has chandeliers, a pillared and swagged bed, a marble fireplace, its original bathroom and a balcony for breakfast. Rooms here are spacious, much as the house's Victorian and Edwardian owners planned them, some of them with fireplaces and big bay windows.

L ike Gravetye Manor, Alexander House is an ideal luxury stop-over, send-off or arrival place for Gatwick airport. Opened in 1987, Alexander House has an opulent feel consistent with the chauffeur-driven, plum-coloured Daimler which can pick guests up at the airport. In part it dates from a seventeenth-century farmhouse. In 1692 the owner's daughter, Helen Bysshe, married Timothy Shelley, forming the conjunction of family names which became more widely known with the works of Helen's grandson, the poet Percy. In 1909 a governor of the Bank of England owned the house and it was he who added the fireplace in the hall, where a welcom-

Alexander House
Turners Hill, West Sussex
RH10 4QD
☎ (0342) 714914/716333)
Proprietor: Roger King
Price grid B

Location: Leave M23 at Exit 10; take A264 to second roundabout; turn right through Crawley Down to Turners Hill; turn left at cross-roads on B2110 and Alexander House is on the left (6 miles from exit 10). By rail to East Grinstead (4 miles). Helicopter pad in grounds.

ing fire is always burning. When he died in 1930, the property, including 740 acres and six farms, was for sale at £30,000! In 1953, the house, known as Fen Place, was opened by the Queen Mother as a retirement home for clergy; in 1984 it was bought by the company which now owns it, renamed after the Chairman, Earl Alexander of Tunis, and became a hotel in 1987.

The rooms are richly gilded and furnished with antiques and paintings and a range of decorations from French ormolu lamps of the nineteenth century to a painting of Jamaica by Noël Coward. The bedrooms have seventeenth-century botanical prints and there are caged love-birds in the lobby area, continuing the bird theme of the fifteen chinoiserie panels in the south drawing room, hand painted on to silk woven to an eighteenth-century design. Mirrors above the Cotswold stone and Siena marble fireplace reflect the chandeliers to infinity.

The twelve bedrooms all have names associated with the house. The Henley suite has a four-poster once owned by a former Prince of Wales and the bed in the Imperial suite is said to have been a gift from Napoleon and is encrusted with ormolu arrows and decorated with the head of Diana. Bathrooms are big, with plenty of fluffy towels, robes and toiletries. Downstairs 'Chalfont' leads off the light oak-panelled library; a cosy L-shaped room around its carved stone fireplace with beams, an ideal spot to take an after-dinner drink from the trolley of rare Armagnacs.

The pastel-shaded dining room is decorated with Italian prints after Raphael, and has tables loaded with Royal Worcester and cutlery bearing the Alexander family arms. The waiters are dressed in an old coachman style of uniform. Vegetarian dishes are available among the seasonal selections. Special picnic hampers can be arranged on request for excursions to the nearby Lingfield and Plumpton racecourses. Alexander House looks out over the Sussex downs, and there are three golf courses in the area which will make special arrangements for

The pillared entrance has been added on to Alexander House.

hotel guests. The hotel has its own tennis court and croquet lawn, and the trout fishery next door has three secluded lakes stocked with brown and rainbow trout.

A treasured memory is of arriving back from Caribbean heat and modern modular hotels to a January shiver of snow and greyness among the hundreds of tall leafless trees (alas, depleted by the gales of October '87) along Gravetye's long drive. Within its sixteenth-century walls, I seemed to have entered a time warp, particularly when going into the Ash room panelled by the first owner, Richard Infield, for his bride Katherine Compton. Their initials, carved in oak over the fireplace, can be seen from the pillows piled high on the four-poster bed. There is something very comforting in the survival of this serene room of wood and antiques. The windows look out over a formal sunken garden. The guest gets another shock passing through the thick walled door to the bathroom, which is in fine Art Deco style. The fourteen rooms all have bathrooms, television, phone and hairdrier, but books and carefully sought-out antiques insulate the guest against too much of today.

Gravetye's seclusion suited eighteenth-century smugglers well as a hideout, but its most notable owner was William Robinson, the gardener who bought the manor and the thousand acres in which it stands in 1884 and lived there till his death in 1935. Here he pioneered the later, much copied, English natural garden idea that is still his memorial in the arrangement of trees, shrubs and the many species of flowers that he continued to plant even from his wheelchair.

· The last time I visited was in a lashing February gale; the yellow glowing light at the end of the drive was welcoming, the champagne and freshly made canapés by the fire my reward for a nasty drive. Fires were, and are, important to the house. Robinson's book *Wood Fires* provides information about fireplaces, firebacks, and special Norwegian stoves for burning birch wood.

Peter Herbert bought Gravetye in 1957 and became a pioneer country house hotel owner. The bedrooms are named after trees on the estate – Robinson would have approved of that – and, although there is central heating, wood fires burn in all the public rooms. The gardens are carefully maintained, rhododendrons and azaleas abound, and autumn stings with colour.

The restaurant echoes the house, with its oak panelling, open fire and candle-light for dinner. A mighty wine list offers a choice of 600

Gravetye Manor
near East Grinstead, West Sussex RH19 4LJ
☎ (0342) 810567
Owner: Peter Herbert.
Member of Relais et Châteaux
Price grid B

Location: 30 miles from London; either take A22 towards Eastbourne and at cross-roads 7 miles past Godstone turn right on to B2028 to Turners Hill; or leave M23 at Exit 10, A264 towards East Grinstead; after 2 miles at roundabout take B2028 towards Haywards Heath and Brighton.
By rail from Victoria to Three Bridges (8 miles from hotel).

The Art Deco-style bathroom contrasts with the Tudor feel of the rest of Gravetye Manor.

wines from classical producing areas, with prices starting at under £10 and soaring to nearly £300 for a 1949 Château Haut Brion. Magnums and half bottles are listed separately; a thoughtful touch. Peter Herbert's son, Leigh, a Cambridge natural sciences graduate, has returned from cooking experience with the Roux Brothers, Huntstrete House, the Rhone vineyards and his own restaurant in Sydney, to be supervisory chef, and has been building up the 1¼ acre kitchen garden with unusual vegetables and herbs. Leigh follows an impressive list of past chefs: Karl Loderer, Michael Quinn O.B.E. and Allan Garth as well as the present chef de cuisine, Mark Raffan. As well as its own greenhouse fruit, soft fruits, vegetables and herbs, Gravetye has its own spring water, apple juice, watercress and free-range eggs. Local game is served, and there are daily deliveries of fresh fish. Leigh's food philosophy is 'satisfying, wholesome and honest, yet light and interesting. Lightness and purity would be my first principles.' Dishes can be sophisticated, such as lightly poached oysters in puff pastry with champagne sauce flavoured with ginger and chives; but through the menus run traditional ideas: 'a warming winter broth', roast saddle of rabbit with saffron sauce and sweetcorn pancakes, medallions of venison, steamed sponge pudding with butterscotch sauce and sautéed apple, traditional blancmange with rose petal syrup. The list of savouries is also rare, but suitable in this setting: for example grilled goat's cheese with croutons and bacon.

Whitehall lives up to its name and has secluded gardens at the rear.

Whitehall lives up to its name, white-washed and funeral card edged in black timbering, overlooking farmland and secluded behind a walled garden with heated swimming pool and tennis court leading from a terrace by the house. Inside, the decor is pastel and modern, with lots of prints, but blends well into the shell of the Elizabethan hall.

Although the property was mentioned in the Domesday Book, the present house was originally built in 1151 for the knights of St John, and the cellars and bar date from this time, the rest from the fifteenth century. After the dissolution of the monasteries, the property eventually passed to Sir Thomas Audley, Lord Chancellor. In the nineteenth century it was owned by the Countess of Warwick, a society hostess and friend of Edward VII. Recently it was the home of Lord 'Rab' Butler, and only became a hotel in 1985. The ten bedrooms are named after Cambridge colleges and are also light, with beams and fireplaces. One room has a cupboard where wigs were kept. There are two rooms on the ground floor for disabled guests.

The chef is 23-year-old Paula Keane, the owners' daughter, who has won guidebook accolades for her cooking (she was the youngest in Britain to receive an Egon Ronay star). The cuisine style is countryfied with dramatic flavour notes; terrine of game will come with a blackcurrant and ginger sauce, and there is a 'menu surprise' of six light courses. Whitehall has its own smoking house for salmon, which is served on fresh salad leaves with a warm poached egg; smoked chicken is mixed with wild mushrooms in a walnut dressing.

Flitwick is a listed manor house set outside the village in the centre of a fifty-acre park with views of river meadows across the lake. The grounds contain a 1780 listed grotto, a ha-ha, an ironstone church dating from the twelfth century, a castellated walled kitchen garden and a wealth of trees and shrubs. The seven-acre gardens also offer tennis, two croquet lawns, trout fishing and a putting green. In spring the woods on one side are full of daffodils and bluebells and huge fragrant yellow azalea bushes. In the walled kitchen garden are chicken runs, beehives and a conservatory with grape vines: a popular place for board meetings. The back yard is the setting for Somerset Moore's collection of veteran tractors and a 1910 Wallis steam traction engine.

From the first greeting by Fifi, the owner's fox terrier, at the end of the 200-yard drive lined with lime trees, Flitwick strikes one as

Whitehall
Church End, Broxted,
Dunmow, Essex CM6 2BZ
☎ (0279) 850603
Owners: Gerard and Marie Keane. Member of Pride of Britain
Price grid B

Location: M25 from London till it joins M11; north to Exit 8 and A120 left towards Broxted. Once in Broxted asking a local is the easiest way of pinpointing the hotel. Helicopter pad.

Flitwick Manor
Flitwick, Bedfordshire
MK45 1AE
☎ (0525) 712242
Owners: Somerset and Hélène Moore
Price grid B

Location: 40 miles from London, Flitwick is quickly reached in as many minutes via M1. Flitwick is signed at Exit 12; follow winding A5120 for 3 miles till the manor appears on the left. By rail from St Pancras on the Bedford line to Flitwick station (½ mile from house), with rail links to Gatwick. 40 minutes from London by train; car collection. Helicopter pad.

pleasantly personalised and relaxed. Green wellies and bikes are available for guests wishing to explore Bedfordshire, England's smallest shire. There is a plenitude of noble houses to view in the vicinity, including Woburn, Ascott, Waddesdon, Luton Hoo; and the Duxford and Shuttleworth collection of rare planes, Whipsnade Zoo and golf at Woburn are also nearby.

The sixteen bedrooms are named after families who have lived in the house. A splendid ground floor room leads to a glassed terrace with television and a view of the garden. A drinks tray is ready set out and a basket of apples. Though there are lovely items around (including jokey ones like wooden apples in a bowl) – 'we don't lock doors,' says Somerset Moore. Many of the upstairs rooms have four-posters and fireplaces. One, 'Fisher', has the best in double bathing, two full-sized baths set together, and the room has a sauna. Bathrooms boast toy boats, wooden detailed models made by Star Yachts in Birkenhead for Moore's previous fish restaurant. The top suite has a roof garden, and 'Albermarle' is in dark green with a huge Italian walnut mirror. The well-furnished rooms are made especially welcoming with books, magazines, guides, board games, hot water bottles, colour television, direct dial phones and hairdriers.

Somerset Moore's French wife, Hélène, looks after the wine list which includes plenty of half-bottles for drivers. The kitchen has an indoor herbery and sea water tank for the seafood that comes from Billingsgate for Geoffry Welch the chef. Since Somerset Moore's previous occupation was running a fish restaurant, the menu not surprisingly is biased

Flitwick's rooms look out on parkland and on to the ironstone church.

towards fish. A speciality is a platter of lobster, crab, prawns, langoustine and a Helford oyster. Other dishes include escabeche, braised turbot, gravlax stuffed with smoked trout, fillets of brill filled with apples and raisins and coated with mild curried sauce, and grilled red mullet with sharp yellow pepper sauce. Dishes are starred on the menu to show low calorie content, and in addition to a seasonal game menu using venison from the Woburn estate, there are set-price shellfish and vegetarian menus.

A country house with a London postal code sounds like a contradiction in terms. But although the hotel is so central, it is approached across Wimbledon Common and surrounded by trees, which gives it a surprisingly rural feeling, especially at night with the Georgian façade picked out in lights.

The house dates from 1727, when its owner was George I's Commissioner of Customs, a gambler and money-lender. Later a governor of the Bank of England and Viscount Melville were owners, the latter planting the trees which still stand in the park. At this time prime minister William Pitt was such a regular visitor that he had his own suite of rooms. In 1817 the owner was a poor but titled Sicilian who luckily married a rich English lady, the daughter of the governor of West Florida. Assuming the somewhat Gilbertian title of Duke of Cannizaro, he and his duchess made the house a venue for musical events.

During the nineteenth century, Cannizaro was owned by Lord Auckland and Maharajah Duleep Singh, but it was a Mrs Schuster who made it a social centre, numbering the Prince and Princess of Wales, Alfred Lord Tennyson, Oscar Wilde and Henry James among her guests. Declining from these heights, the house became an officer's convalescent home in the First World War and recently was a home for the elderly. After it was rescued by its present owners, £3.7 million was spent in restoration before it opened in mid-1987 with 55 bedrooms.

In the public rooms the same country colours are used: soft green, peach and coral, spiked with massive flower arrangements created by a resident florist. The rear windows overlook the 34-acre park, while the front looks towards Wimbledon Common.

Food is styled 'cuisine moderne' and has heavy nouvelle cuisine influence – very pink magret of duck, and plate painting with sauces. The wine list features over 270 vintages, with a wide selection of champagnes. Afternoon tea is served in the lounge and coffee taken around the big fireplace in the hall. A traditional four-course Sunday lunch is available.

Cannizaro House
Westside, Wimbledon Common, London
SW19 4UF
☎ (01) 879 1464
Proprietor: Thistle Hotels
Price grid A

Location: From central London take A3 towards Kingston; at Putney Heath take A219: Wimbledon Park Road, which becomes Parkside; branch right on to B281 Cannizaro Road and Cannizaro Park. By rail to Wimbledon. Hotel cars can be arranged from Heathrow and Gatwick; also limo service to central London; 8 miles from West End.

In front of the carved fireplace under ceiling medallions is the place for afternoon tea at Cannizaro House.

Eight miles south-east of Oxford would not seem to qualify for an 'around London' description, but with motorways M4 linking M25 to M40 within a mile of the door, the Manoir is accessible in around 45 minutes from west London. Many would travel even further, and many do, to sample the cooking of Raymond Blanc, with Anton Mosimann the best-known chef in Britain. He is also – unfairly, considering the joys of tasting his dishes – the slimmest; he was once a model, a perfect size 36, he says. At the age of 19, Blanc was told he was too old to learn professional cooking; boys in France start at 14. Persistence led to a commis waiter's job, which he now feels is essential to understanding the other side of the kitchen door, unappreciated by many chefs. Progress to the stove seemed impossible in France, but in 1975 he took over the cooking at The Rose Revived in Oxfordshire. In 1977 he opened the Quat' Saisons restaurant in outer Oxford, and within a year had gained a *Michelin* star. The Maison Blanc bakery followed, supplying London with real baguettes (the vans now bring back fresh fish for the Manoir). Then the Manoir came along, opening in 1984 with ten bedrooms, a 65-cover restaurant (which now has two *Michelin* stars) and conference facilities for up to 46.

Blanc's reputation as a chef, enhanced by his book *Recipes from Le Manoir aux Quat' Saisons*, for which he received the largest advance ever paid for a cookbook and which is now in its third edition. Great Milton has always been slightly off the London–Oxford main road even in Roman days and it preserves its quietly prosperous tranquillity. A cluster of thatched cottages and the church stand near the Manoir, which was held at the Norman Conquest by the Bishop of Lincoln. Blanc is not the first French owner: a fourteenth-century French Norman noble has the remains of his effigy in the church. In the eighteenth century Great Milton was a rich village supporting a peruke maker and even in mid nineteenth century had four blacksmiths, seven carpenters, two dressmakers, a milliner, a glover, three laundresses,

Le Manoir aux Quat' Saisons
Great Milton, Oxon
OX9 7PD
☎ (0844) 278881/2/3
Owner: Raymond Blanc.
Member of Relais et Châteaux
Price grid A

Location: M40 from London. At Exit 7 for Wallingford and Thame take A329 towards Wallingford; Great Milton Manor is signed on right off A329, and is then on right just before the village of Great Milton.
Notes: Restaurant closed Mondays and Tuesday lunch, and entirely 22 December-19 January. No children under 8 years; no dogs in the hotel, but free kennelling is available in the grounds.

The gardens of the Manoir aux Quat' Saisons are as neat and colourful as its interior.

a surgeon and general practitioner. The Manor's last private owner was Lord Cromwell, who died in 1982.

The multi-gabled Manor sits calmly behind its enclosed walls. It has seven acres of garden and twenty of paddock, and offers riding from its own stables, tennis, croquet, clay pigeon shooting a mile away, and a heated outdoor pool. The gardens are immaculate: lawns fringed with bright flowers; a walled herb and vegetable garden where Blanc grows French seeds for vegetables; he also grows fruit, from which the Manoir's own preserves are made. A surprising feature is the size of the gardens and the splendid water gardens that descend from pools to a stream via a large medieval stew filled with elderly carp.

The dovecote at the Manoir aux Quat' Saisons.

The parlour has a portrait of Charles I, and there is a story that his death warrant was signed there. Sitting rooms overlooking the garden lead off on one side, the two dining-rooms, the Blue Lounge and the Cromwell Room on the other. Upstairs rooms lead off a long windowed corridor and are named after flowers. Each room is supplied with Madeira, and a bowl of exotic fruits. The bathrooms match the colour schemes; four have Jacuzzis. 'Hyacinth' is blue and white, with a canopied bed. 'Madame', the first-floor ladies room, has floral chintzes and a chaise-longue. 'Bluebell', on the floor above, has pretty light window seats and the rooms take on a different character according to the three different building periods of the house.

When the restaurant is closed on Monday and Tuesday, hotel guests can eat from a light room service menu, or enjoy the menu gourmand available on Monday evenings (no à la carte). To dine at the Manoir on Saturday nights one needs to book about six weeks ahead. A three-course lunch menu (not Sundays) is offered at a reasonable price to tempt in new customers. At night there is the *menu gourmand* or seasonal *à la carte*, which can start with delights like slivers of *foie gras* sandwiched between layers of crispy potatoes and turnips with port wine sauce and end with a savoury of crusty twice-baked goat's cheese soufflé with garden salad in hazelnut oil, or a skewer of exotic fruit served warm on iced rice pudding with guava saboyan and passion fruit coulis.

Hartwell is a Grade 1 listed house built between the sixteenth and eighteenth centuries. The Jacobean house was enlarged in 1755, and both the Jacobean and Georgian façades are still in existence. James Gibbs, Henry Keene and James Wyatt all designed for the house. The new owners have carefully restored the window framing in keeping with the periods, and some corner rooms have both styles of window. Old-style top dormer windows have also been replaced and the south façade is reminiscent of a French château.

Hartwell certainly has close connections with France. It was originally owned by a son of William the Conqueror, and later seized by Henry II for his son John, who gave it to the Hartwell family and their cousins the Lees, who were the owners for many years. In 1807 the house was leased to the future Louis XVIII of France, who held his court in exile at Hartwell, where he was joined by the Comte d'Artoise, later Charles X, and the exiled King of Sweden, Gustavus IV. Louis's accession papers were signed in the library at Hartwell, and he then returned to France. In 1938 the house was sold to Ernest Cook, grandson of travel agent Thomas. From 1945 till 1982 the house was a finishing and secretarial school, the House of Citizenship.

When Louis XVIII lived at Hartwell he housed two hundred courtiers in the house, including the Duchesse d'Angoulême, the daughter of Louis XVI, who spent most of her time praying. Now there are 23 double rooms, five single and two with four-posters, and three suites. More suites are projected in the old menagerie building and gardener's cottages. Nearby will be an orangery-style building housing a covered swimming pool, and next door to it a conference room. In Louis's time emigrés short of money opened shops in these outbuildings. The greatest sale of house contents was in the 1930s, when hopeful buyers included Queen Mary, who was served a picnic by liveried footmen in the library.

The huge high rooms of the first floor are named after the King, the Queen and princesses and courtiers of Louis's time; they have spacious sitting areas, unusual pinnacled corner wardrobes and restored cornices and mouldings. The King's room, Louis's bedroom, has a bathroom set behind a false wall behind the fourposter which is decorated with a regal crest. Old brick fireplaces have been uncovered. The sixteenth-century Muniments Room, with its heavily carved panelling and fireplace, is now part of a two-bedroomed suite.

On the upper floor the rooms have dormer windows and lower ceilings, and many of them open on to an unusual roof garden. In Louis's time this was a mini farm, with birds and rabbits and planters full of herbs and vegetables.

New gates are being installed and the approach remodelled so that it sweeps past a

Hartwell House
Oxford Road, Aylesbury, Buckinghamshire HP17 8NL
☎ (0296) 747444
Proprietors: Historic House Hotels. Member of Prestige
Price grid A

Location: M40 to exit 7; A329/418 to Thame; on towards Aylesbury to the village of Stone; continue through the village and Hartwell is signed on left opposite a pub.
By rail from Marylebone to Aylesbury (2 miles).

lead statue of Frederick Prince of Wales (George Lees was a close friend), moved with difficulty from an obscure clump of trees, and past a soaring 1753 Gothic Revival chapel which is now a 'stabilized ruin'. The oriental inspired portico leads to an impressive reception hall with open fire. The rococo style drawing room and pillared Sir John Soane dining room look out over the parkland, and the food will be similar to that served in the other two Historic House Hotels. In the restored library, which has some fine wire and gilt mesh bookcase covers, a portrait of former owner Lisa Lee hangs over the marble fireplace. Off this room, Dr John Lee, another later owner who held temperance festivals in the grounds, had a private observatory, now demolished. The morning room has a superbly moulded ceiling, and a fine carved door and window surrounds. Copies of original paintings of the house and grounds will hang in the public rooms; the originals are on display in the Aylesbury museum.

The 70-acre grounds contain long sweeps of parkland, dotted with eighteenth-century pavilions and statues, laid out by Richard Woods, a follower of Capability Brown. Vistas on the south side lead to an Ionic temple surrounded by four statues. There is a statue of William III but named George II. To the north-east is a large lake stocked with fish, where herons wait hopefully, and around it a walk. It is spanned by the former central section of London's Kew Bridge. A topiary garden planted in 1690 has disappeared, but there are still some dumpy yews that in Louis's day were clipped in the shape of crowns.

The former central section of London's Kew Bridge now spans the lake at Hartwell House.

THE SOUTH EAST

From Cottage to Court

The south-east of England, Kent and Sussex, is a highly populated, prosperous area. Its routes to the Channel Ports have been in constant use since Roman times, and the ancient Pilgrims' Way, leading to Canterbury, is also well trodden. William the Conqueror's success at Battle, near Hastings, changed the royal line. The coast was defended by its Cinque Ports and the sturdy Dover castle, soon to be obsolete when in 1994 the Channel Tunnel brings the area into being as a weekend playground for visitors from the Continent.

In spite of heavy development and criss-crossing of motorways, the south-east retains rural settings which have changed little over the centuries; fields and forests draw the gaze towards the Downs, orchards blossom and bear fruit in Kent, hops are still grown for beer and the visitor can slip back further into the past in country house hotel settings here than in other seemingly less populous regions. The area also has an unusual range of property types where one can sleep: from the five-hundred-year-old beamed cottage and the medieval farmhouse to the noble homes where royals past and present have stayed, and twentieth-century attempts to recreate the past.

A Tudor beamed cottage with roses, foxgloves and clematis round the door, diamond lead windows, duckpond at the back, four-posters and sheepskin rugs in the tiny rooms is an idealistic vision of the English rural dwelling. At Little Hodgeham it becomes reality – provided you book well ahead. Australian-born Erica Wallace fell in love with the house in 1974 when it was derelict, infested with rats, and tree roots pushed through the floor. Having worked in journalism all her life, she was going to open a restaurant. Now recommended and commended by guides and tourist offices, it is a wonderfully tranquil spot to stay. In the garden the weeds have been replaced by flowers, fruit trees and a swimming pool. Inside the cottage, Erica relaid the floors herself, exposed the old beams and in the end did all the building work for £10,000 – half the professional quotations.

Little Hodgeham has only three double bedrooms. One has a stair to a miniature minstrels' gallery with two more beds, another has a four-poster; all have lace and ribbon decorated duvets and pillow cases, and garden flowers are arranged to blend with the colour schemes. Breakfast tray china and bathroom toilet paper are also colour themed where possible. The care Erica takes is reflected in the surge of people to this secluded setting.

Roses round the door greet arrivals at little Hodgeham Cottage.

Previous pages: Tanyard retains the tranquil atmosphere of a fourteenth-century farmhouse.

Little Hodgeham
Bull Lane, Bethersden,
Ashford, Kent TN26 3HE
☎ (0233) 85 323
Owner: Erica Wallace
Price grid C

Location: A20 London–Dover road; right on A28 at Ashford; then right past the village of Bethersden just at Bull Inn; after 2 miles, and cottage is on right-hand side.

Relaxed comfort in Little Hodgeham's sitting room.

She cooks and makes beds for nine hundred visitors a year.

She cooks for her six guests as for a dinner party, even discussing menus with guests when bookings are made, in case of any dislikes. Erica had to fight a local pub in order to get her residential liquor licence. As English as the cottage setting is the breakfast: after fruit or juice there are kippers, scrambled eggs or sausages and tomatoes, and lots of hot toast with dishes of butter, jams and marmalade. Guests can have breakfast in bed and dawdle through the morning or sunbathe by the pool (swimming costumes are available on loan). A free basket containing a Thermos of boiling water, with tea, coffee, milk and sugar, is given to sightseeing guests. The gracious living ideas, Erica says, date from the time when she was brought to Britain to be presented at court: the deb is now a bed and breakfast landlady, mixing elegance with practicality. Dinner is served by Erica in a long skirt, made from old curtains, that hides the flat shoes she wears for comfort when serving. The note on her little brochure sums up the character of Little Hodgeham: 'For free: breakfast in bed, daily Thermos flask, laundry – but iron your own.'

Tanyard is another old country residence that is small (five rooms), but warm and welcoming, and run with housewifely concern for guests' comfort. There does not appear to be a single level surface in this medieval farmhouse dating from 1350. Built as a yeoman's house, it became a tannery. The dining room is a cosy stone-walled room with

The old beamed bedrooms of Tanyard have uneven floors but modern comforts.

tables grouped by a huge open fireplace. There is a four-course set dinner, and the menu changes daily. The rest of the house was added in around 1470.

Even so, all the rooms have private bath or shower room. The second floor has three rooms with bathroom en suite. All the rooms have original old beams and windows, television mounted on the wall or tucked into a walk-in fireplace, and bookshelves under the eaves. Several are decorated with Indian paintings. The sitting room has a big squashy sofa and is filled with books and magazines. Outside there is an acre of garden with a stream running through it and views across the Weald of Kent. Within six miles are Leeds Castle, Sissinghurst, Bodiam Castle and Boughton Monchelsea Place, an Elizabethan manor built in 1567.

K ennel Holt, tucked away in a leafy glade in a wooded valley, is an enchanting find. The beautifully maintained Elizabethan house dates back to 1560. There is a duckpond in front, and the well-groomed gardens include a croquet lawn and a kitchen garden. The Misseldines took over the hotel in 1988 and have furnished it with loving care. The ten bedrooms have television, radio alarm and hairdrier; and iced water, biscuits, hot water bottles and Woods of Windsor toiletries are provided. A little sewing bag (not those fiddly little packets) supplies all the things one needs for repairs while on the move. One bedroom has a rich blue draped four poster; others are decorated in light, pale shades.

Kennel Holt hides itself down a quiet, leafy lane.

Tanyard
Weirton Hill, Boughton Monchelsea, near Maidstone, Kent ME17 4JT
☎ (0622) 44705
Owner: Mrs Jan Davies
Price grid C
Notes: closed 23 December to 1 March (parties of minimum 8 people accepted during that period).

Location: From Maidstone take A229 towards Hastings; turn left at B2163 opposite the Cock Pub; turn right, then first right past Weirton Place country club; branch right and follow winding road down steep hill on to plain; Tanyard is on the left near the bottom.

Kennel Holt Country House Hotel
Cranbrook, Kent TN17 2PT
☎ (0580) 712032
Owners: Mr and Mrs David Misseldine
Price grid C

Location: 50 miles from London, 35 miles from Gatwick. Coming off M25 take A21 south for 20 miles then turn left onto A262 for 6 miles where the hotel is signed; Kennel Holt is down a quiet lane on the right. By rail 1 hour from Charing cross to Staplehurst; collection by car can be arranged.

Downstairs, a room with oak beams serves as sitting room and library, and the front drawing room has a big open fire and chintz sofas, antiques and more beams. The dining room has a chimney-breast in its centre. The Cliffs believe those on holiday should have a good breakfast, and the fresh orange juice is a welcome touch; they also provide afternoon tea and dinner.

Netherfield Place was built in 1924, in Georgian style, and is set in thirty acres of grounds, including a 1½-acre walled kitchen garden and a tennis court. Fruit and flowers are provided in the 14 bedrooms, which are named after families involved in the Battle of Hastings. Rooms have brass bedsteads; one of them 'Mandeville', a huge room stretching the width of the house, has a canopied bed; and even the top-floor rooms are attractively decorated and have breezy South Downs views.

Netherfield has a cocktail bar where afternoon tea can be taken by the fire; on sunny days it is served in the sun lounge or out on the terrace. Michael Collier, a former Savoy chef, is proud of his menus and a wine list containing over 250 vintages. Fish dishes include salmon turbot, filled with crab and served with fresh herb and butter sauce, and smoked salmon accompanied by smoked trout mousse and Japanese seaweed in a watercress sauce; venison is served deglazed with Poire William and coated with a pear and cranberry sauce.

Netherfield Place has sweeping views of the South Downs.

Netherfield Place
Battle, East Sussex
TN33 9PP
☎ (04246) 4455.
Owners: Michael and Helen Collier
Price grid C

Location: 60 miles from London. Take A24 past Tunbridge Wells towards Hastings; right on to A2100 towards Battle; Netherfield Place is on right just before reaching the town.
By rail from London to Battle.

What was once a stop for monks on the way to Canterbury now makes an equally good base for the modern traveller wanting to walk the pilgrims' way – or at least the two miles of it to Canterbury – or spend the night on the way to or from the Continent.

Howfield dates back to 1181, when it was the chapel belonging to the Priory of St Gregory, and the monk's well which can still be seen in the dairy entrance will be a central feature of the new restaurant. The present façade has a faintly Dutch look. Howfield is set in five acres of gardens; there is a magnolia which is impressive in May, and a formal English rose garden. There is also a ten-acre lake. The five bedrooms have been increased to 13 with the addition of a new wing in 1988. Log fires burn in inglenook fireplaces in the sitting room and in the unusual round iron fireplace in the library/TV room. A new bar has been installed in the priest's hole which is now called the Priory Bar. Dinner is served in the beamed, à la carte dining room. The breakfast boasts home-made marmalade and local farm eggs. There is

Howfield Manor
Chartham Hatch,
Canterbury, Kent CT4 7HQ
☎ (0227) 738294
Owner/manager: Martin Towns
Price grid C

Location: Just outside Canterbury. Coming off the M2 take A2 turning at roundabout; after 2 miles turn right to Chartham Hatch through the village 1.3 miles from A2. After another mile down Howfield Lane turn left to Howfield Manor. Alternatively take A28 from Ashford towards Canterbury; 2 miles before Canterbury, and just before a river bridge, turn left and immediately right to the Manor, which overlooks the A28. 53 miles from London.

Howfield Manor near Canterbury has a Dutch look to its exterior.

an all day room service of tea, coffee, afternoon tea and drinks.

This imposing Victorian mansion with its long façade was built in 1883 by Lord Frederick Ducane Godman. It is set in ninety acres of parkland containing rare trees that luckily escaped the worst of the devastation caused by the October '87 storm. Lord Godman was an explorer and botanist, and the many rare azaleas, rhododendrons and camellias – 260 varieties of these shrubs, all tagged – which he planted provide daubs of colour among the taller trees. The garden also contains a magnificent example of a Victorian rock garden. For garden enthusiasts there are other gardens to see in the area, including Leonards Lee, half a mile away, and Nymans. In South Lodge's garden there is a stone from the Great Wall of China set in an architrave to the walled garden where vegetables and soft fruit are grown for the kitchen. Within the grounds, riding, croquet, trout fishing, tennis and clay pigeon shooting are available and there is a golf course at Haywards Heath.

Inside, a passion for trees is demonstrated in the ornate wood panelling and carving, particularly the carved overmantle and shelving in the drawing room.

On his travels Godman collected Oriental tapestries and Islamic pottery and the niches and shelves he created to display them still exist (their original contents were bequeathed to the British Museum; the hotel is gradually filling shelves with suitable pieces, notably in the south-facing dining room.

South Lodge
Lower Beeding, West Sussex RH13 6PS
☎ (040376) 711
Proprietor: Mr Pecorelli. Member of Prestige
General Manager: Bruno Manca
Price grid B. Member of Prestige

Location: On A281 at Lower Beeding south of Horsham. By rail 1¼ hours from London to Lower Beeding.

The 26 bedrooms in the old part of the house are named after rhododendrons and camellias. There are 14 more rooms in converted stables, reached through the old servants' way, where original walls have been exposed in places and the names fit – for example 'Smithy' and 'Farriers'. Here some rooms have steps up to the bed area; bathrooms are in brass and marble with gold plated taps and small television; four bathrooms have Jacuzzis.

The main house has not been structurally changed and the bedrooms are spacious. The 'Earl of Athlone' on the south side, has a superb tiled fireplace; some have split-level bathroom areas. 'Ronnie Corbett' is the nickname for the smallest room, let as a single. Brass door fittings are original, and wood blocks are being made so the crumbling original William Morris wallpaper downstairs can be replaced.

E astwell has a regal history dating back to 1069, and looks suitably impressive. The drive comes sweeping up the hill to an imposing grey stone building with stone partitioned windows and a copse of chimneys balanced by small rounded turrets. Inside, the courtyard is decorated with carved stone walls and the majestic entrance hall has a wide staircase and a vast stone fireplace that looks as if it ought to have an ox roasting in it.

Eastwell gets its name from a spring known to Saxon herdsmen. From the time of William I its owners were royalists. A Tudor supporter discovered Richard Plantagenet, the illegitimate son of Richard III to be among the bricklayers working on the Eastwell estate and,

Rich Victorian panelled interiors welcome guests at South Lodge.

Eastwell Manor
Eastwell Park, Boughton Lees, Ashford, Kent TN25 4HR
☎ (0233 35751)
Proprietors: Norfolk Capital Hotels. Member of Prestige
Price grid B

Location: Leave M20 from London at Ashford exit; take A28 towards Canterbury and first left to Boughton Aluph; the entrance to Eastwell lies beyond the Jacobean gatehouse.
By rail from London to Ashford; ½ hour's drive from Dover.

*A banister sculpture at
Eastwell Manor.*

showing more understanding than most of that
period, arranged for him to spend the rest of his
days in a cottage in the grounds. He died in
1550 and is buried in the Eastwell churchyard.
In Elizabeth I's reign the owner, Sir Moyle
Finch, was allowed to fortify and embattle the
manor house for fear of invasion by the Spanish.
His widow had such an elaborate tomb that it is
now on show in the Victoria and Albert
Museum in London. In Charles II's time
Heneage Finch kept up the mores of the time
by siring 27 children by his four wives – which
kept Eastwell safely in the family for 257 years.

From 1878 to 1898 the house was rented by
Prince Alfred, Duke of Edinburgh, Queen
Victoria's second son. In 1875 Princess Marie
Alexandra Victoria, later Queen of Romania,
was born at Eastwell Manor. She loved the
place, especially the grounds, with its wild
violets and primroses, its Highland cattle and
deer, and before she died wrote: 'However old
I grow the scent of autumn leaves will ever
bring the old English home before my eyes, a
big grey house, in a huge beautiful English park,
woods, great stretches of grass, wide undu-
lating horizons, not grand or austere, but
lovely, quiet, noble – an English home.'

In the 1920s Sir John de Fonblanque Penne-
father – an unforgettable name – tore down the
old building and used the stone to build the
present house, adding in imported architectural
pieces. In 1977 the house was bought by the
Bates family, who renovated it and turned it
into a hotel. The impressive list of past owners
does much to explain the carvings, family
crests, figures on the stair posts and other
decorations, and the 23 rooms bear the names
of former owners. The Middleton suite (named
after the Countess who did much to improve
the estate and woods) has a huge Edwardian
marble bathroom.

Anthony Blake, now at Luckham Park (see
page 71), built up the Eastwell reputation for
food with light, well presented ideas.

The hotel's 62-acre grounds contain formal
terraced gardens, a rose garden, topiary,
fountains and sweeps of spring daffodils. Croquet and tennis are provided; fishing and
shooting by arrangement. The entire Eastwell
estate, some 3,000 acres in all, was described
by Daniel Defoe as being the finest park he had
ever seen.

This lordly, though not over imposing,
house, with its tower and small turrets,
was built in 1850 for the heir of a
wealthy London dyer, Francis Banchard. Its
neo-Gothic style of blue and red patterned
stone was influenced by A. W. N. Pugin,

designer of the House of Lords. Pugin designed the hand-carved oak staircase, a portion of which was shown in the 'medieval court' of the 1851 Great Exhibition. The entrance hall was set off-centre in order to prevent draughts, and to bring light to the main gallery. To emphasize the doorway a tower was built over it. The tiles in the entrance hall are original Minton.

In the 1960s Horsted was the home of Lord Rupert Nevill, Treasurer to Prince Philip. The Nevills spent £1 million on it, and the present owners spent £3 million on restoring original Victorian detail from old drawings. The Royal Family often visited Horsted, and one can sleep in the room used by the Duke of Edinburgh or the Windsor suite where the Queen slept. The rooms have chintzy quilted bed coverings, deep watered silk sofas, Staffordshire china ornaments and Queen-sized beds, and there are fine views out over the downs. The Nevill suite, which was Lady Nevill's room, has an alcoved bed. It has an electrically operated sash window, which can be opened and closed from the bed; apparently Lord and Lady Nevill had differing views on ventilation at night. The Nevill suite's bathroom has three yellow ducks with which to play in the tub. The Tower suite has a sitting room with a spiral staircase leading up to the roof. In case the view of the television from the bed or sitting room is obscured, a second television has been added and all over-head lights have been removed.

There is an indoor pool jutting out into the garden area and a little courtyard garden with a tennis court. There is also a croquet lawn and the Queen's Walk, built by Lady Nevill to enable the Queen to walk to Little Horsted church undisturbed.

The library downstairs has a secret door, disguised by a bookcase, which was designed by Lord Snowdon as a birthday present for Lady Nevill. Eventually the courtyard to which it leads will become a conservatory restaurant (like croquet lawns, something every country house hotel seems to aspire to). The restful double drawing room faces south and the terrace. The blue and white dining room, named after Pugin, is next to the entrance and divided into two by a chimney-breast decorated with the scales of justice (Banchard was a justice of the peace). Chef Keith Mitchell, previously at the Ritz Casino in London and selected for the British team for the next culinary olympics, blends French and English ideas. His desserts are especially notable, and include home-made nougat glacé and hot apple and blackcurrant crumble served with honey-flavoured custard. Hotel residents are automatically members of the Luncheon Club,

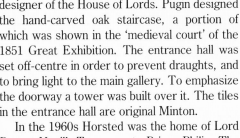

The bird figure on the hand-carved staircase by the Victorian architect Pugin has been adopted as the logo of Horsted Place.

Horsted Place
Little Horsted, Uckfield,
East Sussex TN22 5TS
☎ (082575) 581
Proprietors: Granfell Hotels.
Member of Prestige
Price grid A+

Location: A22 from East Grinstead south through Uckfield; then branch right on to A26 towards Lewes; Horsted Park is on right just after this branch.
By rail, 45 minute commuter service from Victoria to Haywards Heath. Helicopter pad.

The Royal Family were frequent visitors at Horsted Place.

which is also open to outsiders for a small annual fee. Lunch fare includes traditional roasts and sweets such as bread and butter pudding served with double cream and apricot bavarois with a rich brandy sauce. There is also the Horsted salmon and sirloin lunch of sliced smoked salmon, traditional roast beef and Yorkshire pudding, followed by coffee. The breakfast served downstairs is excellent.

Baliffscourt is one of the few country house hotels very near the sea. In William I's time its original titles were Atherington, a village which has now disappeared into the sea, although at exceptionally low tides its remains can still be seen. Baliffscourt is totally unexpected after the rather dreary suburban villa developments of the south coast. Turning down the curving drive one appears to have arrived in a small medieval village. Timbered buildings lean beyond the duck pond in 22 acres of parkland. There are also cottages, including a fifteenth-century gatehouse in which to sleep.

An oak door on huge iron hinges opens on to a small hall containing an iron-bound chest and looking out on to a courtyard, around which there is a maze of rooms, linked by low doorways. The stone around the Gothic mullioned windows is of tawny rough-hewn Somerset stone – a long way from home. The medieval atmosphere seems almost too carefully preserved to be completely authentic. In fact all this was built here only fifty years ago. Lord Moyne spent his fortune, a considerable one derived from Guinness, on this architecturally accurate recreation of a medieval manor. However, it can hardly be dismissed as an utter fake, since he used genuine period pieces of old houses. In the late 1920s, then the Hon. Walter Guinness, he bought a thousand acres of land, on which stood only a ruined Norman chapel and Georgian farmhouse near a moat around the former site of the baliff monk's twelfth-century court house.

When the farmhouse was taken down, the remains of the original courthouse were revealed. All were kept and used in the new house. Stone and timber were imported from other demolished buildings: ceiling beams from a barn in Hertfordshire, a fifteenth-century door from a Somerset stable, sixteenth-century timbers from Surrey, stone arches from a priory, a moulded oak ceiling from a rectory outbuilding. All these were incorporated into the house, built around a courtyard and linked to a secondary building by an underground passage.

While Lord Moyne and his wife toured the

Baliffscourt
Climping, near Littlehampton, West Sussex BN17 5RW
☎ (0903) 723511
Proprietors: Dunham Hotels
Price grid B
Notes: No children under 8 years; dogs £4.75 a day including food and basket.

Location: 60 miles from London. A3 or A24 south from London; continue on A29 where two roads meet to roundabout south of Arundel, take road signed to Ford and Climping and at A259, coastal road, turn right towards Bognor; take first left to Climping Beach, Baliffscourt is on the right.
Helicopter pad.

world in their yacht (later used by the Prince of Wales and Wallis Simpson) looking for furniture and fittings, the Climping locals were both astonished and approving: after all, three hundred craftsmen were needed to rebuild the house. The estate lacked trees, and these too were imported. Two mature woods on the Downs were dug up and replanted.

The surrounding outbuildings were also transplants: a fifteenth-century gatehouse came from North Sussex, strengthened with cement so it could be moved intact; and a seventeenth-century timbered house was moved from Basingstoke. The Norman chapel, used at various times as dairy, cellar – beer kegs on the altar – party room and maid's bedroom, was restored to more reverential duties and is now occasionally used as a private theatre. The perpetrators of this historical amalgamation did not have long to enjoy the result of the three years' work. Lady Moyne died only a few months after the building was finished, and Lord Moyne was assassinated by the Stern Gang while a minister in the Middle East in 1944. Their ashes are buried in the Norman chapel.

Since 1948 Baliffscourt has been a hotel but has preserved its historical Jacob's coat dignity well. Flemish and French tapestries hang on the walls bought by Phillips as a fire damaged museum lot and rewoven to the imagined design. The original doors remain, but the desire for historical accuracy has not prevented guests from being provided with private bathrooms, direct dial telephones, television and radio in the rooms. Eight of the bedrooms have four-posters and in nine rooms it is even

Baliffscourt looks as if it has been there since the middle ages but was actually reconstructed in the 1920s.

possible to light a log fire. There are many unusual features in the bedrooms. 'Bayliss', the old master suite has twin baths; 'Arondelle' has its bed in the window; 'Wymcrofte' has crewel work covers for the four poster; 'Tattesham' has stone window-seats.

In the bar there are oak settles and decorative old bottles. The dining room has a wooden ceiling, Gothic stone windows, superb panelling hung with copper pans and a somewhat macabre medical chest which is said to have belonged to Nelson. The menus are reproduced in Old Style lettering making it difficult to read. The dishes at lunchime go much for traditional English cooking. However, there are also slices of calves' liver bound in a light honey and pink grapefruit sauce, and best end of lamb has a lime sabayon on a rich port wine sauce. The evening menu is based on French cuisine. On fine days, meals can be taken in the courtyard beneath the rambling roses or in the walled garden. Guests' appetites are sharpened by the walks on private paths to the shingled beach protected by the National Trust. Climping beach is ideal for windsurfing and there are three nearby golf clubs. The park contains a swimming pool, tennis courts, a croquet lawn and a 'tee to green' area; riding on the Downs can be arranged in Arundel.

The card room at Baliffscourt.

Sir Edwin Lutyens was another architect who looked back to past architectural delights and put his inimitable design on them. At some of his houses his work was complemented by that of gardener Gertrude Jekyll. Little Thakeham is one of their collaborations which are now country house hotels, the other being Greywalls, near Edinburgh (see page 171).

Little Thakeham's exterior suggests a larger manor house than it actually is. Both front and rear aspects have lovely stone gables, and the small leaded windows at the rear look out over orchards and the Downs beyond. Like the large stone entrance hall, the gallery above, which the Ractliffs hope to turn into a display area for works of art, is spacious and has the bedrooms leading off it. The house was designed for family living and the names of rooms reflect their former uses. The Ractliffs have endeavoured to find Lutyens period or style pieces of furniture to complement the setting, and the minimum of alterations have been made. For example, the Day Nursery next to the Night Nursery, still has a tiny window at floor level looking out on to the garden. Lutyens put it there so that a child left in its cot would have something to look out at. Here too the bathroom has been ingeniously fashioned

Little Thakeham
Merrywood Lane,
Storrington, West Sussex
☎ (09066) 4416/7
Owners: Tim and Pauline Ractliff. Member of Pride of Britain.
Price grid B.

Location: From London take A24 road towards Worthing; 1½ miles after the village of Ashington turn right off the dual carriageway and follow lane for 1 mile; then turn right to Merrywood Lane and Little Thakeham is 300 yards on the right.

Little Thakeham, a Lutyens gem in southern England.

within one of the huge chimney-breasts – probably Britain's only hotel bathroom inside a chimney. It is a large room with a day bed and a huge mirror piped with fabric to match the bed quilt and canopy.

Downstairs a huge Palladian hall with a minstrels' gallery and double height bay windows is popular for receptions. The bar has an immense red-brick walk-in fireplace, as big as a cottage room, containing chairs and a huge flower arrangement. Framed racing photos dot the tables; Tim Ractliff owns a successful racehorse. The dining room, original in design, has a Lutyens sideboard with heavy hinges next to the former fireplace. Diners sit on Ambrose Heal chairs, which are still being made in oak to this 1902 design. The menus change daily, though lamb, local game and fish from Selsey are always featured. Fran Smith, the chef, has been at Little Thakeham since its opening and provides 'straightforward not clever food' on a small but flavoursome menu which can include parsnip and apple soup, hot smoked haddock with prawn mousse, and grilled calves' liver with gin and lime sauce.

The gardens have been somewhat modified since the Jekyll era of plentiful gardeners. The Ractliffs, only the third owners of the house, have reduced the borders, and narrowed some of the flower-beds, but have retained the long rose pergola above the sunken croquet lawn. Azaleas and maples add colour. The devastation caused by the severe October '87 storm that shifted four thousand tiles and damaged some old trees has been cleared up and the serene orchard and Downland outlook smoothed out again. Tennis, croquet, swimming (in a tucked-away heated pool), archery and clay pigeon shooting are available, and the Ractliffs are hoping to organize shooting house parties. The horse enthusiast will find not only a sympathetic host but easy access to the racecourses of Goodwood, Plumpton and Fontwell; while there is polo to be seen at Cowdray Park and show jumping at Hickstead, just 14 miles away.

Lutyen's attention to detail can be seen even in the door locks at Little Thakeham.

THE SOUTH
Hardy Country Hideaways

The staircase at Tylney Hall.

The fast M3 motorway leads to Hampshire and its historic attractions: the old capital of Winchester, with the longest naved cathedral in England, the repository of Saxon royals; the New Forest, its 145 enclosed square miles a royal hunting ground in Norman times; and small yachting harbours to its south. The Forest is superb either for walking or for riding. It has small towns like Ringwood, Lyndhurst and Lymington, with its Georgian high street; Beaulieu, with its motor museum; and Bucklers Hard, where the wooden battleships of Nelson's and earlier navies were built.

It is literary country. Dickens was born in Portsmouth; Conan Doyle worked there as a doctor and lived in the New Forest at Minstead, which is also famous for the Trusty Servant pub, once a haunt of the forest gypsies. Jane Austen's house is at Chawton, near Alton; Marryatt wrote *The Children of the New Forest* at Chewton Glen; in Lyndhurst churchyard lies Alice Hargreaves, the inspiration of *Alice in Wonderland*; and naturalist Gilbert White wrote about his beloved plants at Selbourne.

All over Dorset there are reminders of the novels of Thomas Hardy. A county that is only just being 'discovered', still rural and sleepy, so much so it has been used for film settings of Agatha Christie novels set in the 1940s. In Dorchester, Hardy's 'Casterbridge', there is a statue of the author, and it was here, in this traditional county town, that he worked as an architect. Hardy's birthplace at Bockhampton can be visited, now in the hands of the National Trust. Shaftesbury, with views over Blackmoor Vale, was 'Shaston' in *Jude the Obscure*. Sherborne, with its castle built by Sir Walter Raleigh, was 'Sherton Abbas' in *The Woodlanders*. Eggardon Hill, near Maiden Newton, was used for the filming of *Far from the Madding Crowd*; and Bournemouth was 'Sandbourne' in both *Jude* and *Tess of the d'Urbervilles*: this was where Tess lived with Alec d'Urberville and eventually murdered him. Many more Hardy trails can be followed from country house hotels in the area, and the West Country Tourist Board issue a helpful leaflet on Thomas Hardy's Wessex.

At Evershot, where Summer Lodge is set (see page 63), on the ancient Ridgeway you can see 'Tess Cottage', where Hardy's heroine stopped to ask for a drink of water on her way to Beaminster. There are lovely walks to be made through Melbury Park to Melbury Osmond among grazing horses and deer. Leading down from Chedington (see page 61) through Beaminster to the coast is the 'hidden valley': here there are prehistoric forts, unchanged, unploughed fields, water-mills, apple

Previous pages: Lainston House is set among lime and chestnut rides.

orchards once used for cider, and splendid houses such as Parnham, the Tudor mansion where John Makepeace and his craftsmen produce high-quality furniture, and rare wild flowers and badgers are found in the woods around Hooke.

Tylney Hall, listed grade II, has an imposing drive to a red-brick house. Leading away from the large terrace at the back is a long avenue, said to offer the longest uninterrupted view in Hampshire. The Tylney family owned the house in the 1700s and a great deal of land around it, but the original house was pulled down in 1898, and the land bought by Sir Lionel Phillips who rebuilt the house between 1899 and 1902 – a building described by Nikolaus Pevsner as conservative for its date. The smoking room's moulded ceiling was copied from a sixteenth-century room but even more impressive is the Great Hall, partly panelled in Italian walnut, and with a stone fireplace and Italian ceiling brought in sections from a palace in Florence.

After hospital service in the First World War, when the park was used as an army mule base, it was bought first by Lord Windlesham and then in 1919 by Major Cayzer, the Clan Line shipping magnate, later Lord Rotherwick. In 1953 the hall became a school, and in October 1985, after £3 million had been spent on renovation, it reopened as a hotel.

Sixty-six acres of land are still attached to the hall. Sir Lionel Phillips had them laid out by architect Robert Weir Schultz, who followed the ideas of the Arts and Crafts movement of

Tylney Hall is said to have the longest uninterrupted view in Hampshire from its drawing room windows.

Tylney Hall
Rotherwick, near Hook,
Hampshire RG27 9AJ
☎ (0256) 724881
Proprietors: Deepdene
Hotels. Member of Prestige
Price grid B

Location: M3 from London to
Junction 5; A887 to
Basingstoke; at crossroads
with A30 take signed road to
Rotherwick, through
Newnham; Tylney Hall is
then on left after 1 mile.
By rail from Waterloo to
Hook or Basingstoke, and
taxi to hotel.
Helicopter pad.

the time. He consulted Gertrude Jekyll on some of the detailed planting. Now the lines of the Italian garden are being restored, and the water gardens drained and dredged.

Tylney has 36 bedrooms in the main house and a further 55 are being added in two courtyard areas, along with an indoor pool and gym. The hotel aims to house conferences and offer special weekend packages such as Gilbert and Sullivan workshops, wine breaks and Christmas house parties.

Stephen Hine, who trained at the Dorchester and worked at Prue Leith's restaurant in London and Oakley Court, produces light country flavours; a roast each evening is carved from the trolley in the hotel's conservatory-style restaurant. Menu notes are fillet of brill wrapped in ginger and lettuce, steamed, and served with a light orange and vegetable sauce; floating islands with cinnamon cream, and English farmhouse cheese-board.

Indoors work offs include the billiard room, outdoors a heated pool, tennis courts and croquet lawn. The Tylney park golf club neighbours with 18 hole course, archery, and clay pigeon shooting. Hot air ballooning, riding and fishing can be arranged.

In spite of its splendid-sounding title, Fifehead is a cosy informal house on the main road, with a croquet lawn to the side of the house and gardens in which to sit out. It is a place for cat lovers. Large sleepy house cats lounge around, and the walls are hung with enchanting cat prints.

'The Wallops' is considered such an amusing name for a group of villages, and these are such pretty places, meandering through a valley, that they rate their own sign off the Winchester Road. Fishing lessons can be taken on the River Test, and riding and walking are among pastimes offered. Local sights include Stonehenge which is a 15-minute drive away, and the Museum of Army Flying at Middle Wallop. Not far from the hotel is the iron-age fort at Danebury, where you can sometimes watch the archeologists at work. Less ancient souvenirs may be found in the dozen or so antique shops at Stockbridge, five miles away.

Wallop does not mean what one imagines. It is said to be Saxon for 'stream on the hillside' or 'place of the ancient Briton'. Both apply equally; the Anglo-Saxons built a settlement here in the sixth century; 500 years later it belonged to Earl Harold, whose wife Godiva was noted for her horsemanship in Coventry. She lived where Fifehead Manor now stands. Her son Harold, later defeated by William I at Hastings, owned the neighbouring manor at Over Wallop. By the

A carved stone in the grounds at Fifehead Manor.

Fifehead Manor
Middle Wallop, Stockbridge, Hampshire SO20 8EG
☎ (0264) 781565
Owner: Mrs M. Van Veelen
Price grid C

Location: From London take M3 to Junction 8; then A303 towards Andover; left on to A343 to Middle Wallop; Fifehead is on the crossroads with the A272 Winchester road.

fourteenth century the name of the village had become Wallop Fifhide, referring to the five hides of land paid to knights in return for a pledge to provide men to fight for the king; five hides were about 600 acres, and until 1847 the manor had around 575 acres.

Fifehead's dining room, formerly the main hall, is supposed to date from the eleventh century and once had a gallery. Priests used a ledge inside the Tudor chimney-stack as a hiding-place during the Reformation hunts. The mullioned windows are mid-fifteenth-century and the smaller fireplace is Jacobean. Though little remains of the huge original manor, Mrs Van Veelen as owner has the right to call herself 'lord of the manor'.

Now the atmosphere is hardly lordly, for the staff are young and friendly. Dinner is served by candle-light in the beamed dining room, with its leaded windows, and displays of old glass and silver over the fireplace. Chef Mathew Beard buys produce daily and often gives it seasonal themes. Smoked cured salmon comes grilled on oak leaf and lamb's lettuce, with a tomato and basil dressing; there is a terrine of ratatouille and a hot crab tart with red pepper sauce.

The 17 bedrooms (including six singles with shower rooms) are furnished in light pastel florals.

T he entrance drive of Lainston House curves half a mile up a tree-lined hill, through 63 acres of parkland, and circles round to the house's entrance court on a ridge. The Georgian-style windows and dining room

Fifehead Manor was once the home of Lady Godiva.

The octagonal dovecot at Lainston House.

gaze down long rides of lime and chestnuts garlanded with mistletoe and footed in spring with snowdrops, later daffodils. Beyond are the south Downs.

The house dates from the seventeenth century, when the owner Philip Meadows was Latin secretary to Oliver Cromwell and diarist John Evelyn visited and admired the garden, noting the pond for the horses and the well with a wheel turned by a donkey. A later mistress of the house was a lot more lively. Elizabeth Chudleigh, a maid of honour to Augusta, Princess of Wales, seems demure and serene in her portrait hanging in the hall, but she led a very liberated life. She married a young naval officer, the grandson of the Earl of Bristol, secretly at night in 1744 in Lainston's church. Later she became the mistress and then the wife of the Duke of Kingston and was tried for bigamy in Westminster Hall. She took off for Europe and in the course of her travels set up a brandy factory in Russia.

Other Lainston owners also had their moments of notoriety. Mentioned in the Domesday Book, Lainston was then set aside for the monks of the Priory of St Swithin, Winchester Cathedral's saint, whose day in July sets the pattern, it is thought, for the English summer's weather. One Lainston owner was imprisoned for forgery; another hanged at Newgate prison, and in the nineteenth century for ten years the house became an asylum for 96 lunatics. In 1980 the house was converted to a hotel. Plaster cornices were copied and replaced, wooden panels matched, and fire and plumbing needs blended in to the general William and Mary setting. The chunky radiators in passages and hall were rescued from a hospital in Whitechapel. Fourteen new rooms were added in the Chudleigh wing. The first-floor rooms in the main house are high ceilinged, while the cosy upper rooms under the eaves have dormer windows and exposed beams.

Four rooms have been more recently added in a single-storey wing which balances the Chudleigh wing; they are tucked away behind the façade of the eighteenth-century loggia. These suites have French windows giving on to the lawn, which is convenient for croquet, breakfast in summer and walks to the ruins of the twelfth-century chapel (said to be haunted by Lady Chudleigh), near which is a dogs' cemetery. Former owners were keen huntsmen, and one with a withered leg was high sheriff of Hampshire and president of the Hampshire hunt. An 1898 picture of the hunt meet at Lainston hangs in the hall, contrasting with a photograph of a similar one taken in 1986 and one of a coronation celebration for Edward

Lainston House
Sparsholt, Winchester, Hampshire SO21 2LT
☎ (0962) 63588
Proprietor: Pennyplain Hotels
General Manager: Richard Fannon. Member of Prestige
Price grid B
Notes dogs by prior arrangement; facilities for the disabled.

Location: Take M3 to Winchester then A272 Winchester/Stockbridge road; 2½ miles from Winchester, Lainston House is signed at Sparsholt; the entrance is a few hundred yards along the Sparsholt road.
By rail from London Waterloo to Winchester.
Helicopter pad.

VII taken in 1902 in Sparsholt village. Today the hotel will arrange shooting parties on local farmland though clay pigeon shooting in parkland fields near the entrance is more often available. In addition to an eighteenth-century dovecot, the grounds contain a herb garden and tennis courts, while golf and riding can be found nearby.

The 32 rooms are serviced by 54 staff, and there is a 24-hour room service. The entrance hall has the welcome of a log fire set in an eighteenth-century Delft tiled surround and there is a similar one in the suite above. The drawing room runs the width of the house and has two fireplaces and deep, chintz-covered chairs. Opening off this is the Cedar room, a small bar which was once a library; the wood from a single cedar tree, which fell in the grounds in 1930 was used to panel it. The dining room is the former family dining room and nursery. German-born chef Frederick Litty has been at Lainston since it became a hotel, and gives a Continental touch to local Hampshire produce such as watercress, trout, meats and game. Specialities include smoked salmon with hazlenut and lemon dressing, cheese pancake with apple purée, veal with wild mushroom stuffing and Madeira sauce, and country fruit jar of seasonal berries marinated in red wine. Vegetarians are served a variety of dishes, including fresh noodles with pepper and mushrooms in a light cream sauce flavoured with nutmeg.

Half a mile off the road past many grazing horses, the original manor dates from the eleventh century and was used as a hunting lodge by William II. Around 1666 Charles II hunted here in the company of Nell Gwynn, and his coat of arms decorates the panelling in the fifteenth-century dining room – today the oldest part of the house. The New Forest fallow deer seen in the grounds were bred from a pair Charles II brought back from his exile in France. He also doubled the amount of timber supplied by the Forest for the Navy and 270 of New Park's trees were marked by the admiralty for use at Bucklers Hard to build men o'war. The manor was later the principal residence in the Forest, until adapted to be a hotel in 1970. The forest motifs in the form of acorns and oak leaves appear on door furniture and fireplaces, a commemoration of the debt Charles II owed to the oak tree which hid him from Cromwell's men when he fled to France.

The entrance is modern; added with the wing of ten black and red themed rooms. The old house is a maze of staircases and rooms on different levels. Some have four-posters, and

New Park Manor Hotel and Stables
Brockenhurst, New Forest, Hampshire SO42 7QH
☎ (0590) 23467
Proprietor: Kiln Power Ltd.
Price grid C
Notes dogs allowed in a number of bedrooms at a daily charge. Stabling available for horses.

Location: From the M3 take M27 to Cadnam, Junction 1; go south on A337 through Lyndhurst towards Brockenhurst; New Park is on the right roughly half-way between the two towns (5 miles form M27). Southampton 9 miles.

families and their pets are welcome (even budgies have stayed). There are some larger family rooms with window-seats overlooking the swimming pool. One room has stained-glass windows. Attic rooms have creaking, uneven floors. The corridors, with red carpet and often smelling of food, are depressing, but the rooms are welcoming, if a little shabby.

Ciro Peleiccio, born in Britain of Italian parents, was formerly chef at Stocks Hotel. He uses seasonal forest produce such as venison, and the menu includes home-made soups, sea fish terrine, and main courses of guinea fowl, shark steaks with light lobster sauce, and vegetable curry. The dining room has pink decor, tall windows, a beamed ceiling and a panelled fireplace bearing the royal arms.

The stables founded by Charles II were later adapted to the horses and carriages of the manor, and are now riding stables. Those booking riding holidays are given accommodation on bargain break or bed and breakfast terms, with meals as required, and riding is at a reduced price for hotel residents. Tuition and rides are for all levels, and handicapped riders are given special attention. Instruction is also given in stable management and the care of horse and equipment, and the stables take part in local gymkhanas and shows. The Rhinefield Polo Club welcomes visitors from the stable, and has games every Saturday from the end of April to the end of September. The manor also organizes 'interesting breaks' through the year, devoted to subjects ranging from gardens, (which includes entrance to local attractions such as Stourhead and the Hillier arboretum near Winchester); and heritage, with visits to Stourhead, Beaulieu, Broadlands (the home of the Mountbattens at Romsey), Wilton House and Kingston Lacy; to walking in the New Forest and along the coast.

Chewton Glen is, dare one say it, perfect. In fact one critic even complained that it was too excellent. To list all its accolades would take too long; guests can read the press eulogies framed in the hotel billiard room. It is remarkable that standards have never dropped since 1966 when Martin Skan opened Chewton Glen evolved from a derelict house. In those days, says Skan, no one went to a country house hotel, even though the era of the seaside resort was already at an end. Early profits were ploughed back into the hotel fabric, and since then the hotel has never rested on its very gilded laurels; fabrics, prints and carpets are continually upgraded, and bathrooms renewed, long before they seem to need it. The latest additions are a conservatory-style res-

Charles II once had a hunting lodge at New Park Manor.

taurant, not to cram in more people but to give more table space and privacy, and a golf course of nine par 3 holes reserved entirely for guests. In the near future Skan is planning to build a health club in a lower field, out of sight of the house. It will have a swimming pool and indoor tennis, with professional coaching available. Intended primarily for hotel guests, it will also have a limited outside membership. Chewton already has an outdoor terrace pool, with waiter service, and a croquet lawn (where the hoops have to be rapidly removed when helicopters come in). Chauffeur-driven house cars can take guests on one- or two-day tours to Bath, the New Forest, Dorset and Longleat, among other places. In this way the guests can sample the 400-plus listed wines without any worries.

The house gets its name from a deep wooded chine, with the Walkford brook running through it, that is known as Chewton Denny, a ten-minute walk from the hotel. The stream has a bed of greenish clay, in which shark's teeth have been found. The cliffs of sticky earth by the shingle beach are somewhat unlovely, but geologically of international importance, and fossil hunters can be seen scouring the silt.

Two hundred years ago the beach nearby was used by smugglers for entry into the New Forest. Chewton itself can be traced back to the Normans and has been a manor in its own right since 1316, though it is thought that building only began on the present site in 1732. In the 1840s the house belonged to the brother of Captain Frederick Marryat, and it had a Nash-style Georgian façade with a verandah in the days when the author of *Children of the New Forest* stayed there. Now the hotel rooms are named after characters from his novels, and books and mementoes of Marryat are displayed in the hotel. In the early twentieth century brick façades were added in the Queen Anne style popularized by Victorian architect R. Norman Shaw. The bar (recently redecorated by Nina Campbell) was then a vinery, shown on Victorian photos hung in the hotel. In 1947 the house and 1500 acres failed to reach a reserve sale price of £15,000!

The courtyard gives on to an entrance hall with Turkish rugs and a constantly burning fire. Staff materialize in anticipation of the mood and needs of the traveller. Tea and sympathy, a glass of champagne and a menu to study, or just peace and quiet in your room, where a decanter of sherry is provided and there are biscuits to nibble. Even a tray of tea has thoughtful touches: the choice of brown or white sugar, and padded paper holders for the hot handle of the pot. Complimentary in-house movies are shown on televisions housed in chests of

Dried flowers in an alcove in the bar at Chewton Glen.

Chewton Glen
New Milton, Hampshire
BH25 6QS
☎ (04252) 5341
Owner: Martin Skan. A member of Relais et Châteaux and Prestige
Price grid A
Notes no children under 7 years. Kennels near the hotel.

Location: From London take the M3, then the M27 to Bournemouth; take the A337 to Lyndhurst; after Lyndhurst take A35 towards Bournemouth. After ten miles (ignoring signs to New Milton) pass East Close hotel on left and turn left at sign to Walkford and Highcliffe opposite the Cat and Fiddle pub; go through Walkford, take second left 'Chewton farm road', and turn right into Chewton Glen drive. By rail, London Waterloo to New Milton, 5 minutes from hotel, who will arrange collection. Helicopter pad.

An immaculate croquet lawn at Chewton Glen.

drawers; rheostat-controlled lighting sets the mood; and for peaceful sleep there are individual quilts on the double beds.

The hotel service can cope like a skilled juggler with many simultaneous events, to the detriment of none. One late spring morning I watched a model being photographed with golf clubs for a new brochure, senior oil executives in discussion over their coffee on the terrace, American guests sipping drinks by the pool, as chauffeurs tended their cars (the hotel cleans windscreens every day for guests), and Jilly Cooper arrived for a lunch given by her publisher; then a bride arrived by helicopter on the croquet lawn, her dress billowing in the slipstream, to be met by a tail-coated toastmaster, scarlet against the immaculate green lawn and clashing horribly with the azaleas, who swept her and her guests into a private reception. Yet my room-service lunch arrived promptly, exquisitely presented.

Such smoothness only comes with hard work and does not come cheap. Rooms are decorated to suit their differing sizes and shapes; in each case the theme is taken from the prints on the wall, which come from a shop in Bath, and to which papers and fabrics are matched. Ideas abound: a roll of padded fabric cushions a low bathroom beam, protecting the taller guest's head and adding a decorative feature. Bathrooms have non-slip floors and decorative baskets of dried flowers made by a lady in the New Forest; some have sunken baths with padded arm- and head-rests; the Marryat suite has a sunken bath for two. Showers are separate where possible and double basins included. The coach-house and stable block, where the old manger still survives, contain new rooms which will eventually have balconies. Some are split-level suites with a private patio secluded behind hedges, and their own parking space.

The good food rates a *Michelin* star. Chef Pierre Chevillard worked with the Troisgros in France and has been at Chewton for eight years. There are salads and light luncheon suggestions, and smoked salmon can be ordered as a main course. Other dishes include a hot mousse of fennel and wild mushrooms; Dorset veal with lasagne and lime sauce; scorpion fish steak in red wine sauce with bone marrow; and individual tropical fruit soufflés or poached pears in red wine sauce scented with bay leaf. Set menus, and good house wine at £6.50 a bottle, with halves and magnums available, make Chewton more affordable.

Maiden Newton's grounds run down to the mill leet of the River Frome.

Chewton Glen is a hard act to follow, even in a book, but Maiden Newton can take up the challenge quite easily. It is quite small (three double, two single rooms, and two more projected), and essentially a private house hosted by its resident owners. They don't use the word 'hotel' on their brochures; nor does the atmosphere suggest one. The house is set in a delightfully quiet part of the village with croquet and other lawns running down to the mill leet of the River Frome. There is fishing, free to guests, on a private ¾-mile stretch of stream stocked with brown trout – 'small but good'. Daily and weekly licences are available from the Ferrisses, who provide rods and fishing maps for the use of their guests. Any catch can be cooked for breakfast or frozen to take home.

Guests eat together in a dining room decorated with huge antique cheese covers. The wine list is short (29 items), but Bryan's selections are good. 'The dinner party atmosphere pulls it together,' they say.

The house was built in 1846, but using stone from a medieval house, so it looks older, with its mullioned and leaded windows and tall chimneys. It was owned by the grandson of a Dorset poet admired by Hardy, and the house is briefly mentioned in *Tess of the d'Urbervilles*. The bedrooms have traditional country antiques. The Trellis room has a specially made painted half-tester with new firm mattresses (the Ferrisses sleep in all their guest rooms in turn to make sure they are comfortable). Old tubs are used in some of the bathrooms, and welcome touches include an 'emergency box' of travellers' needs, home-made shortbread biscuits by the bed, and tea-makers with a choice of Darjeeling, Lapsang and camomile teas. Elizabeth keeps spare pyjamas and nightdresses to lend to forgetful guests, and also sells tights. The biggest room, named William Scott, after the builder of the house, has a four-poster with a spotlight at the bed-head for reading in bed – and there are plenty of books around the house. The bathroom contains Elizabeth's exercise bike. Guests' names are hand written on white cards on the bedroom doors.

The menus offer no choice but are

Maiden Newton House
Maiden Newton, near Dorchester, Dorset
☎ (0300) 20336
Owners: Bryan and Elizabeth Ferriss.
Price grid C
Notes closed January; no children under 12 years; no dogs in public rooms.

Location: From Dorchester take A356 road towards Crewkerne; in village of Maiden Newton (very traffic choked) turn right by Spar grocery store and up a little lane towards the church; Maiden Newton House is on the left opposite the church.

The gardens at Maiden Newton soften the old stone work.

announced far enough in advance for pet hates to be eliminated. The Georgian table is set with Minton china, flowers, silver and crystal. Local products are used where possible; even a Dorset wine is listed. The cheeseboard is all West Country, with types like Sharpham, Devon Garland, Dorset Blue Vinny, and Capricorn from Crewkerne; and cheeses are also available for guests to buy to take home. Pre-dinner drinks are taken in the drawing room on a help yourself basis. A typical dinner would be watercress cream and tomato yoghurt, haunch of venison roast with juniper berries, ginger and red wine, always with four fresh vegetables, followed by rhubarb fool or baked cheesecake brulée, cheese, coffee and chocolates.

Older children can have an earlier, lighter dinner and the Ferrisses encourage guests to invite their friends for dinner. They also want to revive the exclusive house party and would welcome groups of 10-12 people who would take the whole house while the Ferrisses did all the housework and cooking.

Having made the house beautiful with their own porcelain, paintings and antiques, the Ferrisses are restoring the gardens. There are lawns on three sides, and the church to the north. There are some 400-year-old yews and long, high yew hedges. The walled garden is filled with spring bulbs, and a newly planted 140-foot rose walk divided in two by an ornamental fishpond. The house has a grand piano and a library for dull days, and apart from the trout fishing and 21 acres of their own rough shooting there is also hunting with the Cattistock, and coastal fishing in Lyme Bay.

A happy feature of this house is that it has been in the same Prideaux-Brune family since the early seventeenth century, and since 1973 has been run as a 'restaurant with bedrooms' supervised by the family. There are now twelve rooms; six in the manor and six in a converted stone barn in the grounds, though the owners stress that the restaurant is still the mainstay of the business.

Built by Charles Brune in 1665 of local stone, the house is surrounded by lawns with croquet and tennis and skirted by the Devenish stream, a tributary of the River Stour. A painting of the original house partly destroyed by fire in the eighteenth century hangs by the stair. The two-roomed dining area can accommodate sixty people at one sitting and is only open for dinner (closed Sundays and Mondays from November to March). Three four-course set menus are served, featuring country dishes such as cucumber and soft

Plumber Manor
Sturminster Newton, Dorset
DT10 2AF
☎ (0258) 72507
Owners: Richard and Alison Prideaux-Brune; *Chef:* Brian Prideaux-Brune.
Member of Pride of Britain
Price grid C
Notes closed February; free horse stabling; no children under 12 years or pets.

Location: From Blandford Forum take A357 towards Wincanton; Plumber Manor is 2 miles south-west of Sturminster Newton on the Hazelbury Bryan road.
By rail to Gillingham, Dorset.

The dining room at Plumber Manor.

cheese mousse, salmon mousseline with dill and white wine sauce, and breast of chicken with Stilton mousse and port sauce; and a vegetarian main course is also available.

The bedrooms in the main house lead off a gallery decorated with family portraits. Some of the rooms have fireplaces; all have private bathroom, television and tea-maker. The bathrooms are large, and have window-seats from which to watch the Devenish go by. Light fabrics have been used and stable style doors open on to a courtyard for sitting out. In winter with specially reduced breaks, hair driers and umbrellas are provided to cope with weather, and shooting parties come in winter. Free stabling with straw and water is available on a do-it-yourself basis for guests who wish to hunt with local packs, and a full livery service can be arranged nearby.

Chedington and the Chedington family were on record here in 1316 but the present house was built in 1840 and the large estate around it was broken up in 1949. Thomas Hardy knew the area well, and the Chapmans keep a collection of his books in the house. He wrote of the inn at Winyards Gap, mentioning landmarks near Chedington: 'There you see half south Wessex, Combe and Glen, And down to Lewsdon Hill and Pilsdon Pen'.

An author could hardly improve on some of the local village names. Cricket St John, Brympton d'Evercy, Sandford Orcas and Lytes Cary sound like settings for an Agatha Christie or P. G. Wodehouse novel. From the outside Chedington Court has a Jacobean look, with its

Chedington Court has gardens terraced down to the River Parrett.

pinacles and chimneys in mellowed stone; tall trees providing seclusion, the gardens descending at the back in richly planted terraces. The interior, however, seems to belong more to the P. G. Wodehouse era, in spite of moulded ceilings and heavy Jacobean-style furniture in the entrance hall. The afternoons here tend to consist of croquet or putting, reading in the summer house or the huge, well-supplied library, a self-service drink in the billiard room before pre-dinner drinks.

Upstairs the rooms vary in size and decor. 'Dorset' is the 'best' room, with a huge bay window; 'Rhododendron' has a big window seat; 'Devon' a Dutch inlaid bed; 'Thomas Hardy' and 'William Barnes' (the Dorset poet Hardy admired) are rooms on the second floor with beams and sloping floors. One room, 'Queen Mary', has furniture and a carpet that came from the liner, including the bed, the wardrobe and a lovely dressing table. These were introduced in the 1950s, when the house was owned by a shipping man. Another boat-mad man, Peter de Savary (see page 185), spent some of his childhood living here.

Breakfast, says Philip Chapman, is 'anything you like'. In fine weather it can be taken at leisure (as can dinner) in the high-roofed Victorian conservatory. The cooking is done by Hilary Chapman, who has been termed a 'cook's cook' and who used to run a restaurant in Somerset. Dinner is a five-course affair, with home-made soups and a trolley of desserts and cheese. The wine list contains over five hundred wines from around the world, and sensibly includes about a hundred in half-bottles. All

Chedington Court
Chedington, Beaminster, Dorset DT8 3HY
☎ (0935) 89265
Owners: Philip and Hilary Chapman. Member of Relais du Silence and Romantik Hotels
Price grid C (includes dinner).

Location: M3 and A303 from London towards Ilminster; B3165 left to Crewkerne; A356 to Dorchester; turn right at top of hill to Chedington Court, about ½ mile down on right in trees. By rail from London Waterloo to Crewkerne, or from Paddington to Taunton; trains can be met. Helicopter pad.

kinds of diets can be catered for. Philip markets, then Hilary plans the menu according to what is freshly available. Guests are summoned to dinner table by table, to eat by candlelight, and classical music plays in the background.

The ten-acre gardens slope down towards the valley. They contain a duckpond with a thatched duck house, little summer houses for snoozing in, secluded lawns and mellow terrace walks trailed with roses. There are mature trees, rounded topiary, old yew hedges and stone steps leading down to quiet walks. The River Parrett rises here, creating a pond which feeds the water garden.

Summer Lodge has won big acclaim in its ten years of existence. Once the dower house for the Earls of Ilchester, it is a small cosy Georgian house of no great architectural or historical interest other than that Thomas Hardy in his architectural capacity designed the drawing room. The glimpses of superb flower arrangements through the large drawing-room windows as one goes up the short drive prepare the visitor for its pretty, flower-filled interior.

Cats lounge by the log fire; flowers and collections of old cheese dishes decorate the rooms. The bedrooms are furnished simply with candlewick bedspreads and look out on the garden or the village roofs. The well tended garden has a heated swimming pool for use in summer, and the Lodge is a good base for walking. There are wonderful views in this area, and Batscombe Hill is home in spring to

Summer Lodge
Evershot, Dorset DT2 0JR
☎ (0935) 83424
Owners: Nigel and Margaret Corbett
Price grid C (includes dinner)
Notes closed usually in December; no children under 8 years; small dogs by prior arrangement for small charge, but not allowed in public rooms.

Location: Take the A356 (see above), Evershot is signed on the right opposite Beaminster turning; Summer Lodge is signed as you come into the village.

The rooms at Summer Lodge have views of the gardens.

primroses and violets, and later wild orchids. Within a 25-mile radius, there are ten golf clubs as well as hunting with the Cattistock, riding from nearby stables, and trout lakes for fishermen. There is also the fascination of detecting spots used in Hardy novels. Evershot itself was 'Evershead' in *Tess*, and at the top of Evershot high street near the Acorn inn is 'Tess Cottage', where the heroine called to ask for a glass of water. The chimes of St Osmond's church remind one of time passing, and St John's Hill, behind the church, is the source of the river Frome, which we met at Maiden Newton and which will meander into the next chapter. On the edge of the village is Melbury House, with its deer park, that Hardy used as his model for 'King's Hinstock Court'.

Back at Summer Lodge, Margaret Corbett provides *cordon bleu* cookery. Her set dinner menus are based on local produce and feature local cheeses such as Dorset Blue Vinny served with crisp Dorset knobs – small round pieces of dried bread. The traditional ways of making blue vinny (a corruption of veiny) are not approved of now. To produce the blue mould, farm workers would dip their horse's harness in the milk churn at the end of the day, or leave old harnesses or boots in the dairy; nowadays injected spore is used. It is a difficult cheese to make, and has to be hunted down almost with secrecy. Other more prolific local cheeses served at Summer Lodge include cheddar supplied by Mrs Montgomery, a local farmer's wife, and goat's cheese from Somerset.

The dishes are straightforward English favourites like smoked salmon with scrambled egg, cheese and onion quiche, potted shrimps, dressed crab, steak kidney and mushroom pie, local game, lamb and rainbow trout and good old country puddings: Tipsy sherry trifle, banana lime syllabub, apple amber, Duke of Cambridge tart and lots of fruit variations, with fresh fruit salad with pineapple and kirsch always available.

Behind its creeper cladding and tubs of flowers, Bishopstrow has a plush and contented feel that reminds one of a sleek cat and seems to fit its ecclesiastically lordly name; Warminster is a centre for Church of England training. The house, at the top of a drive cushioned in spring with banks of violets, was built in 1817 by John Pinch of Bath. The entrance hall is more like a drawing room, with its huge mirrors, nineteenth-century oil paintings, a mixture of English and French antiques and Persian carpets.

The staircase rising beside a mighty hanging lamp leads to 26 rooms, all opulently furnished and equipped with television. High buttoned

The entrance to creeper-clad Bishopstrow House.

Bishopstrow House
Warminster, Wiltshire
BA12 9HH
☎ (0985) 212312
Owners: Blandy Brothers.
Price grid B

Location: M4 from London; take A36 Bath turn-off and continue through Warminster; Bishopstrow is then on left just after the town; or M3 to A303; continue on this to A36 right turn; the hotel is on the right before reaching Warminster. (Follow signs to Bishopstrow.)

Probably the most sumptuous indoor hotel pool in Britain at Bishopstrow House.

bed-backs are made regal with swags and canopies of fabric, richly echoed in curtains and bedside table cloths; pelmeting and Austrian blinds also consume bolts more of fabric, more French in style than the usual English chintzes. The Oval Room has a canopied bed, superb carpets and a marble bathroom. Some of the bathrooms have Jacuzzi; one is pillared and has an oval Jacuzzi bath and gold swan neck taps, potted palms and a pleated silk ceiling.

In spite of the rich, warm interiors, the house has a light indoor/outdoor feel. This is partly due to the presence of probably the most magnificent indoor pool in any British country house hotel. It is large with tall arched windows along one side, and a pillared portico filled with potted parlour palms and cane chairs. There is also an outdoor pool and both indoor and outdoor tennis courts, sauna and solarium. You can walk down to the River Wylye, where you can fish for trout on the hotel's own river bank; there is golf 1½ miles away and stately homes to visit nearby: Longleat, Stourhead, Wilton House and Laycock Abbey among them.

The conservatory-style dining room adds another garden touch to the interior, and there is also an outdoor terrace for eating out on warm days. The dining room with more parlour palms is in white paintwork; its tall window, pale blinds and tall white candles on the tables suggest Italy or the south of France rather than Wiltshire. The chef is Chris Suter whose menus include three salmon dishes (smoked, marinaded and fresh Scottish salmon served with a chive sauce), a fricasée of rabbit and braised, stuffed pig's trotters.

THE WEST COUNTRY

Water is Best

The gateway to England's West Country is the serene golden stone city of Bath. Developed by the Romans, who appreciated the hot sulphurous spa waters that Dickens' Mr Pickwick later said 'tasted of warm flat irons', Bath can be called Britain's first holiday centre. Its popularity was revived in the seventeenth century, when Samuel Pepys remarked, 'It cannot be clean to go so many bodies together in the same water.' But in the next century Beau Nash built the Pump Room and inscribed over its portals in Greek: 'Water is best'. The consequences of not heeding this advice and of eating and drinking too heavily drew Society to Bath, and London mothers hopefully brought their unmarried daughters to be seen eating at the Pump Room.

The fashionable draw of Bath led to the building of comfortable solid square country houses within a few miles radius. Today several of these homes have become country house hotels.

Plunging further west into Devon, the wilderness of Dartmoor contrasts with the neat calm of Bath, its surrounding Mendip Hills and the cathedral city of Wells.

Around Bath the country has a mysterious haunted feel. King Arthur's legends cast their shadow on its hills and deep valleys. Glastonbury, said to be the place of burial of King Arthur and Queen Guinevere, is also associated with Joseph of Arimathea, who on his travels struck his staff into the ground at Glastonbury: taking its flowering as a sign that his travels were at an end, he founded what is thought to be the first Christian community in England.

Many sailors, and now retired folk from the Midlands and the North, find on coming to the West Country that their travels are over. Plymouth is the port from where Sir Francis Drake watched the Armada approach 400 years ago. Near here are sea-wracked cliffs and deep harbours and the little island of Burgh, containing the only private island country house hotel.

Ston Easton, a grade I listed Palladian mansion, may look rather forbidding with its formal Georgian exterior but behind the elegant façade is a story of a labour of love by Peter and Christine Smedley. The love affair began when they first saw Ston Easton during a gale in 1977, two-thirds derelict, with a ladder in place of the staircase, and walls and ceilings missing. Next day, in autumn sunshine, they committed themselves to restoring it. Their bid was accepted in five minutes. They sold property in Scotland and London and poured money into what Christine Smedley now describes as a 'black hole of expenditure'. That,

Previous pages: Burgh Island has been described as a temple to Art Deco; the glass-domed palm court epitomises this with its Lloyd Loom chairs.

The elegant Georgian salon of Ston Easton Park has been restored carefully in period.

accountants insisted, had to stop, and so the hotel idea evolved. For almost nine months in 1982 the Smedleys ran the hotel themselves, yet won an award for the 'hotel of the year'. Now they have managerial help, but insist that they want the house to be as unlike a hotel as possible. No one is encouraged to use the bedroom keys and there is no bar; drinks are served as and when guests require them.

The Smedleys spend one or two months each year trying out each guest room in turn and noting any faults, such as worn light fittings and loose handles. Once Christine was disturbed by the ringing of the phone from a neighbouring room and had a massive wall rebuilt to improve the sound insulation. Four rooms have recently been refurbished at a cost of £70,000, which included installing a pair of porcelain parrots made by the Marchioness of Aberdeen and Tremair on eighteenth-century carved brackets over a genuine Chippendale wardrobe in the Master Suite; the parrots tone with the National Trust fabric used in the room. Four of the bathrooms were once 'powder rooms', used for the preparation of wigs. Four-posters dating from Hepplewhite and Chippendale periods have day sofas at their foot. Each room has plenty of armchairs or sofas in which to relax. Some have canopy wardrobes like crusader tents and 'Ludlow' is said to be haunted by the ghost of the housekeeper who murdered the still room maid.

The severe exterior contrasts with the interior's rich mouldings on doors and walls. The salon has canvas paintings simulating stone or stucco reliefs, and the door is flanked by

Ston Easton Park
Ston Easton, Bath,
Somerset BA3 4DF
☎ (076121) 631
Owners: Peter and Christine Smedley. Member of Pride of Britain
Price grid A
Notes no children under 12 years; free kennelling for dogs by arrangement on the premises; pets not allowed in the hotel bedrooms or public rooms.

Location: Take M4 to Junction 18; take the A46 to Bath and then the A4 (A39). Ston Easton Park is signed on the A37 on the left past A39 cross-roads; Bath and Bristol 11 miles.
By rail from Paddington to Bath.

The listed Georgian entrance facade of Ston Easton.

Corinthian columns and pediment. The ceiling shows the eagle of Jupiter descending out of the sun – all restored and repainted in eighteenth-century style under the guidance of Jean Munro, an expert on the period. The drawing room is lighter and has a French feel, its ceiling decorated with garlands of flowers and ribbons. This room was used as part of a French château setting for a Maigret television series. The library has an open fire and mahogany book-library has an open fire and mahogany book-cases, the Print Room next door is fitted with cupboards, decorated with eighteenth-century engravings pasted on the walls and 'hung' with garlands in the style of the time.

Ston Easton gets its name from the strata of stone running along the Mendip Hills. The Hippesley-Coxe family were the houses' principal owners, entertaining William Pitt the Younger. In the nineteenth century, Lady Hippesley-Coxe family were the house's principal owners, entertaining William Pitt the making in the east wing. It was so odorous that her husband had the room walled off from the house. This lady also had a plunge bath in an octagonal room under a domed ceiling studded with gold stars. Surrounded by statues, the bath had steps leading down to it. This room still exists, although the bath is now beneath the floor. By 1958 permission was sought to demolish the deteriorating building, and a grant of £15,000 was offered to anyone who would take on the house, but no one would. In 1964 Lord William Rees-Mogg bought the house and rebuilt the roof.

Downstairs you can see the early kitchen, linen room, game room, still room, wine cellars and billiard room, some of which give glimpses of life 'below stairs' in the eighteenth century. Camellias border the entrance, but the 25-acre gardens are on the grand scale of Humphry Repton. He transformed the 'dark silent pool' behind and below the house into a wide river broken up by cascades to create a fast-running stream spanned by little bridges. The approaches, the tree planting and wooded walks are all to Repton's plans. Overlooking the stream are mature oaks, yews, willows, green and copper beeches, and the garden contains wells, a ruined eighteenth-century ice house, and a sham castle folly next to the gardener's cottage where the Smedleys now live. One can admire the house from Repton's river with a picnic hamper of patés, quiche, smoked salmon, quail's eggs, strawberries and clotted cream, local farmhouse Cheddar from nearby Chewton Mendip with Bath Olivers (named after Bath spa's first physician in Beau Nash's day who devised the dry biscuits as a diet food) and house wine or champagne. After that, a little croquet or billiards is a pleasant way to pass the afternoon.

The more energetic can hire cycles or take a horse out on the Mendips, but the best views of all are from a hot-air balloon. There is a one-hour flight, which takes off from the park, followed by a champagne picnic.

Welsh-born chef Mark Harrington supplies a good table in the Old Parlour. The Smedleys, however, know that many visitors on a tour of country house hotels have stomachs weary of too much good food; and if anyone just wants a poached egg on toast they are happy to provide it. Nevertheless it would be a shame to pass up Harrington's baked fillet of salmon wrapped in filo pastry and sorrel; or hot baked chocolate pudding with English custard, a sauce too many chefs seem ashamed of presenting, or hot bread-and-butter pudding with apricot sauce. On Sundays there is a traditional choice of lunch roasts; and the breakfast menu will include haddock, kedgeree and grilled kippers.

In 1715 a visitor to the home of a rich Quaker clothier wrote, 'This day went to Lucknam, it being the day of Mr Wallis's (the owner) birth on which he arrived at full age, there was a Great Entertainment and much company. I stay'd there all night.' Much the same can be said of the house today, following its opening as a hotel in 1988. It has not yet, however, put on the fête champêtre for eight hundred people, the inhabitants of Colerne, with which the wedding of the owner to a daughter of one of Nelson's captains was

Lucknam Park is set in a 270-acre estate and has its own springs and water tower.

celebrated. The firing of the cannon commenced the feast, and a sketch of the scene is in the hotel scrapbook. A twentieth-century owner, Sir Alfred Read, chairman of Coast Lines, removed the dark oak interiors and restored the Georgian look, and there has now been further redecoration along authentic period lines.

Lucknam is seen at its most impressive when approached up the mile-long beech avenue through the 270-acre estate, the trees framing the pillared and gabled central façade. Next to the hotel is a stud farm; its champions include Raffingore, who held the world speed record for a racehorse in the 1960s. The restoration work was done by Longs of Bath, the firm who converted the Pump Room at the turn of the century. A total of 39 bedrooms have been made, many in mews style in the old stable and coach-house block at the back, which together with a large health centre forms a sheltered courtyard area. The ground-floor rooms here are suitable for the disabled. The Roman-style leisure spa, which has a private membership but is free to hotel residents, includes a solarium with stereo, beauty treatments, massage, exercise bicycles, steam room, sauna, snooker room and heated indoor pool, as well as an outdoor sun terrace and a small restaurant serving light snacks all through the day.

Next to this area is a walled, formal garden with an eighteenth-century dovecot. There is croquet, tennis, archery, and a jogging track; hot air ballooning and shooting are available, and you can hunt with the Beaufort. The spacious rooms are furnished with antiques and have Italian marble bathrooms; one, the Romeo and Juliet suite, has a balcony and its own garden. There is a library with trolley bar service, plenty of open fires (with a resident fireman to tend them) two restaurants presided over by executive chef Anthony Blake, formerly at Eastwell Manor in Kent (see page 39), and a wine list of over 300 labels. Produce comes from a kitchen garden, and the house has its own water springs and water tower. A harpist plays while you eat, and recital dinners will be held in winter.

The Dovecot in Lucknam's garden.

Lucknam Park
Colerne, Wiltshire SN14 8AZ
☎ (0225) 742777
Proprietors: Lucknam Park Hotels
Director: Christopher Cole.
Member of Prestige
Price grid B
Notes local kennel arrangements for dogs.

Location: M4 to Junction 17; A4 to Chippenham and through to Batheaston, 2 miles, left for Colerne through village; Lucknam Park is on left 15 minutes from Bath (6 miles), 1½ hours London.
By rail from London Paddington to Bath. Chauffeur-driven cars can be arranged for collection from arrival airports. Helicopter pad.

C ombe Grove Manor is another house in the Bath area which has taken advantage of the space it possesses to install a spa leisure facility (after all, that was Bath's original attraction). Here it is the separately housed Cannons Country Club. (When asked for directions, locals seem to know this better than the manor house hotel, which opened at the end of 1987.) Hotel guests can use the club

The hall at Combe Grove Manor has typical Georgian decoration of the Bath area.

facilities, such as the large gym, aerobics and dance studio, sauna, solarium, indoor pool, sun terraces and outdoor heated pool. It also has tennis (floodlit), squash and 5-hole par 3 golf, with tuition available in all three. There are jogging and nature trails in the 68 acres of woodlands and gardens, where deer, badgers and foxes may be glimpsed. From the ten-bedroomed 1780 manor set above the village of Monkton Combe there are views over its five acres of formal terraced gardens and along sixteen miles of the Limpley Stoke valley to the White Horse at Westbury. In 1781 Combe Grove was described by the *Bath Chronicle* as having a greenhouse, pleasant gardens and a kitchen garden, walled and well stocked 'with the dearest fruit trees now in their prime.' There is a nineteenth-century Bath stone pond with five hundred goldfish near the entrance gates.

John Wesley preached in the courtyard at Combe Grove and pronounced the house 'congenial and relaxing'. Today guests who climb the fine two-tiered balustraded staircase can relax in comfortable rooms with beds canopied and draped, enjoy the alcoved baths, and unwind in Jacuzzis; half the rooms are designated non-smoking. Downstairs the rooms are high-ceilinged and light, and the eye is drawn towards the view, which can also be enjoyed from the long narrow dining room where Raymond Dufy, formerly at Bath's Royal Crescent Hotel, prepares his set menus. His ideas include fresh scallop-filled ravioli with chive sauce and chicken *quenelles* with *foie gras* in fresh tarragon sauce.

Combe Grove Manor
Brassknocker Hill, Monkton Combe, Bath BA2 7HS
☎ (0225) 834644
Proprietors: the Jack Chia group of companies
Price grid B

Location: 2 miles from the centre of Bath, 12 miles from Junction 18 of M4; take A46 to Bath; A36 out towards Monkton Combe; turn right at Brassknocker Hill (steep) between Combe Down and Monkton Combe.
By rail from London Paddington to Bath; car collection by arrangement.

If you are anxious to know what a rich seventeenth-century landowner kept in his manor house, you can find out at Huntstrete House, where there are parchment copies of a 1646 document listing the estate inventory for their owner Sir Francis Popham (the same family held the house till 1956). The document was found at Littlecote, prior to its sale to Peter de Savary, a house also once owned by the Popham family. The Huntstrete inventory notes 'in the greate dineing room 4 peaces of arras hangings . . . item, a bell to ringe to prayers . . . item, one Syder presse and a yoating stone'. (No one knows what the last was used for.)

Today 'items' are more likely to be paintings by Thea Dupays and the £½ million spent in 1986 alone on antiques and a new dining room. The dining room has nine chefs under Bob Elsmore, who worked with Mosimann at the Dorchester and at Buckland Manor (see page 98). The seasonal menus include salmon from the Wye, Devon lobster, pheasant and partridge in winter; and the large kitchen gardens supply much of the fruit and vegetables, as well as flowers. The dishes, in spite of Elsmore's work in France, are very English; soups come with croutons; jacket-baked potatoes are included in the vegetable selection; puddings include shortbread tart filled with lemon cream, bread-and-butter pudding with warm vanilla sauce, passion-fruit posset, and cheeses include local Chewton Mendip Cheddar.

Hunstrete stands on a hill and is approached through its own park. In its present form the house is largely eighteenth-century. In 1987 it won a RIBA architectural commendation for conversion of the eighteenth-century coach-house and stables into rooms and its new dining room. The latter is built as a terrace; it has chandeliers and creamy decor, and its arched windows look out on an Italianate styled courtyard. The public rooms are well lined with bookshelves, even in the hall area where a ginger cat sleeps in the chairs where coffee and afternoon tea are served. The 21 bedrooms (soon to be 24) are named after birds and have four-posters or brass or canopied beds, all with drapes and spreads in rich fabrics. In the courtyard area, Swallow Cottage has a bedroom, a bathroom, and a sitting room with a small fireplace for a quiet retreat.

The garden contains a croquet lawn and a tennis court; flower-beds lead to an old walled garden crossed by raised grass paths, and the vegetable beds are bordered, unusually by rose trees. The gardens are a source of inspiration for Thea Dupays' paintings. The heated swimming pool is in a corner of the walled garden,

Huntstrete House
Chelwood, near Bristol,
Avon BS18 4NS
☎ (07618) 578/9
Owners: John and Thea
Dupays. Member of Relais et
Châteaux.
Price grid B
Notes no children under 9
years; no dogs.

Location: 2½ hours from
London taking Exit 18 off
M4; A46 to Bath; A4 from
Bath towards Bristol; after
about 4 miles, at the end of a
short dual carriageway
stretch, turn south (left) on
to A39/A368 towards Wells
and Weston super Mare;
continue for 4 miles to
Marksbury; turn left on to
A39, but continue on A368
(straight on); take first right
towards Huntstrete village;
the entrance to Huntstrete
House is on left and signed.
Chauffered cars from the
airport can be arranged.

The flowers in the gardens inspire the owner Thea Dupay's paintings at Huntstrete House.

beyond which is the vegetable garden and paddock, where free-range chickens provide eggs. Riding is available at stables in Huntstrete village, a five-minute walk away, and trout fishing and golf are also nearby. Hot-air ballooning from the grounds can be arranged.

Comfort in a Victorian house setting at Homewood Park.

Compared to the stately eighteenth-century stone piles round Bath, Homewood is a grey Victorian house with a 1984 addition in which the eaves are already home to swifts and swallows. It is surrounded by ten acres of informal gardens, a two-acre vegetable garden and there is croquet, tennis and pleasant walks from the grounds into the Limpley Stoke valley. The entrance has a pillared portico and the windows have Gothic pretensions, but it is the sense of warmth and hospitality (it was 1987 hotel of the year) rather than historical associations that endears Homewood to guests. It does have a pedigree, however: the site was once occupied by the abbot's house belonging to the adjoining thirteenth-century Hinton Priory, of which the fourteenth-century cellar walls and dining-room walls are the only remains.

Penny Ross favours blues and apricots in her colour schemes, and the 18 bedrooms have been furnished with great attention to detail. Room 12, for example, has pine corner wardrobes, floral bedspreads, cloth covered bedside tables with lamps which are good to read by, and floral cushions hang from a rail behind the bed to make reading more comfortable. In the bay windows there are chairs and a table with flowers, sherry, plenty of postcards and writing paper.

Penny also looks after the garden. The hotel is virtually self-sufficient in summer produce, and bowls of fruit are set out in the corridors for guests to help themselves. Stephen, who worked with Kenneth Bell at Thornbury (see page 93) and then set up Popjoys restaurant in Bath, is in charge of the kitchen. Meals are served in the pink clothed (pink is the house colour) dining room, candle lit for dinner. His menus may include watercress pancakes filled

Homewood Park Hotel
Hinton Charterhouse, Bath, Avon BA3 6BB
☎ (022 122) 3731
Owners: Stephen and Penny Ross
Price grid B
Notes closed Christmas Eve to mid-January.

Location: leave M4 at Exit 18; A46 to Bath; A36 towards Salisbury; just before Hinton Charterhouse turning on the right, take left turn to Freshford; Homewood Park is on the left not far up this road. Bath 5 miles.

with crab and orange butter sauce; leek and potato soup with croutons, unpuréed and delicious; chinese leaf and mussel soup; ragout of scallops and monkfish with leeks and saffron; and desserts such as blackberry and apple crumble and *oeufs à la neige* with Grand Marnier and custard. Stephen calls his menus 'contemporary English', and vegetables come in generous portions. The Rosses have recently opened a hotel in an old house in Bath, called Queensbury House.

L ike Selwood Manor (below) Burghope is a private family house. Built in 1270, it has been in Elizabeth Denning's family since 1309. It was opened six years ago to overnight guests. The Dennings, finding themselves in charge of a 718-year-old house, 'with bits falling off continually', founded the Heritage Circle in 1981. Now there are about thirty stately home owners, who take in guests rather than let their homes become cold museums.

Burghope's ancestry has associations with Archbishop Cranmer, and the sitting room has a huge fireplace engraved with Elizabethan biblical quotations. The outstanding features are a rare mosaic-tiled floor, and a priest's hole; while low doorways, ships timber beaming, thick walls, a fifteenth-century drawing room with leaded glass windows and utter quiet are most characteristic of the house.

Guests are met by the Dennings on arrival, perhaps with tea in the elegant sitting room looking out on the walled gardens. During the stay guests get plenty of opportunity to ask for advice on sightseeing and day trips, as well as

Burghope Manor
Winsley, Bradford on Avon, Wiltshire BA15 2LB
☎ (022 122) 3557
Owners: John and Elizabeth Denning. Founder members of Heritage Circle.
Price grid C

Location: leave M4 at Exit 18; A46 to Bath; A36 towards Salisbury; 5 miles from Bath, with Viaduct Hotel on the right, turn left on to B3108 to Winsley and Bradford on Avon, under railway bridge and up hill to Winsley village; *immediately* after 30 mph restriction signs turn left into small lane marked 'except for access', the high walls surrounding Burghope are on the left; follow along lane to entrance. By rail to Bath or Chippenham.

Biblical quotations from Elizabethan times over the fireplace at Burghope Manor.

which local pubs to go to for lunch. In addition to hosting shooting parties in season, the Dennings also arrange four-night tours of stately homes in different parts of Britain, in which each tour uses one country home as a base for the four nights. The tour at Burghope would include day visits to Sheldon Manor, dinner with the Duke and Duchess of Somerset at Bradley House, and a private tour of Longleat, with dinner hosted by Lord Christopher Thynne.

Dining at Burghope is a special occasion in the beamed dining room, candlelight trembling on the family silver, with all house guests, family and their invited friends sitting together. John Denning looks after the wine (included in the dinner price) and stimulates conversation with his extrovert stories, while Elizabeth serves 'typically English food'. Roast beef, pheasant, salmon and fresh local produce are the backbone of the menu.

Selwood is a peaceful haven not far from the centre of Frome. It is a listed Jacobean house built in 1622 by John Selwood, a rich wool merchant at a time when Frome was a prosperous wool centre. Set in 14 acres along the River Frome, with its own coarse fishing rights, a small herd of Jacob sheep and herb garden, the house is long and low with old beams, original staircase, big stone fireplaces filled with wood-burning stoves, and mullioned windows. But each room has its own private bathroom, television, radio and central heating, and there is a heated swimming pool, a croquet lawn and clay pigeon shooting. Up to 14

Selwood Manor
Frome, Somerset BA11 3NL
☎ (0373) 63605
Owners: John and Valerie Chorley
Price grid B

Location: 30 miles from M4. Take A362 from Frome towards Radstock for 1¼ miles; as the road rises to a bend, turn right down a small lane; Selwood Manor is 400 yards on the right.
By rail from London Paddington to Bath Spa.

The gardens of Selwood Manor are manicured and colourful.

people can stay and like Burghope the house is open year round even at Christmas. Adjoining the house is a cottage dating from the eighteenth century with two bedrooms, one bathroom and an eating area. Guests can choose to have dinner served here; otherwise it is taken in the main house, either together or separately, according to choice. Four-course dinners are served by arrangement, and menu selection can cover sole and smoked salmon terrine, with pink Hollandaise sauce, shellfish *mille feuille*, *poussin* (spring chicken) with lemon and fresh herbs, salmon mayonnaise, saddle of lamb with garlic and rosemary, Concorde cake (chocolate meringue and chocolate mousse), or *creme brûlée* with grapes. Dover sole is always available as well as steaks. The cook, Mrs Crofts, is cordon bleu trained and formerly owned and ran the Hoops Inn at Bideford.

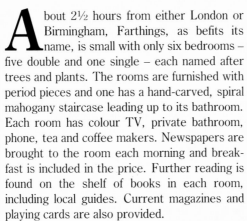

Farthings Country House Hotel at Hatch Beauchamp.

About 2½ hours from either London or Birmingham, Farthings, as befits its name, is small with only six bedrooms – five double and one single – each named after trees and plants. The rooms are furnished with period pieces and one has a hand-carved, spiral mahogany staircase leading up to its bathroom. Each room has colour TV, private bathroom, phone, tea and coffee makers. Newspapers are brought to the room each morning and breakfast is included in the price. Further reading is found on the shelf of books in each room, including local guides. Current magazines and playing cards are also provided.

The local guides give information on the wealth of places to visit. The hotel is conveniently set to explore Exmoor National Park, the Quantock and Blackdown hills; the latter very nearby and once the inspiration for Wordsworth and Coleridge. There are riding stables in the next village and four golf courses within a ten-mile radius. Taunton, the home of cider, and Wells, with its spectacular cathedral, are within easy reach and, using the M5, Exeter and Bath are not far afield.

Set in the centre of a quiet village, the 200-year-old house is set in three acres of secluded gardens with plenty of sheltered spots for sitting out. Supervised by Claire Cooper, meals are prepared by a young chef, Wendy Bate, who formerly worked at Huntstrete House. Four-course set menus with plenty of selections, changed every month, are served for dinner; and the restaurant is open to non residents. Lunches are only served by arrangement for residents and picnics will be made up for guests who want to explore the surrounding countryside. The kitchen uses local produce with an emphasis on English and French recipes.

Farthings Country House Hotel
Hatch Beauchamp, Somerset TA3 6SG
☎ (0823) 480664
Owners: George and Claire Cooper
Price grid B
Note Dogs and children by arrangement

Location: Take A303 past Ilminster, right onto A358 to Hatch Beauchamp; alternatively hotel is four miles from the M5 Junction 25 on A358.

The River Teign runs through the gardens of Gidleigh Park.

These precise directions are necessary in deepest Dartmoor. The plunge from Chagford with high, leafy, car width lanes means no U-turns and just tunnelling on encouraged by signs which say 'keep going, you're not too far away now' till the lane narrows to views of Gidleigh. This is certainly not a place for the bright lights, but a base from which to enjoy walking the hotel's forty acres, where there is tennis, croquet or riding in the park. Whether you are walking or riding, the hotel will, given notice, arrange for a guide to go with you; it also organizes special walking breaks in the winter.

After a day on the moor the wonderful *Michelin*-starred cooking of Shaun Hill is a just reward. For each meal at Gidleigh a 25p surcharge is added (unless the guest objects) to be sent as a donation to the Dartmoor Preservation Association. Shaun Hill, one of the few Britons in the Académie Culinaire de France, has been made a director of the hotel. His food principle is 'keep it simple'. He buys fresh produce, particularly game, and collects wild mushrooms in the surrounding forests. He dry-cures beef in the kitchen and makes his own preserves. China is hung on the walls of the restaurant, which is two small pink-tone rooms overlooking the water gardens. Flavour combinations and ideas are eclectic: warm partridge mousse with morel mushroom sauce; roast corn-fed pigeon with herb *foie gras* ravioli. Each day a set dinner of two courses with cheese and dessert can be selected from a list which changes daily.

Paul Henderson admits that the main Gidleigh interest is food and wine. He is a natural host, with no previous hotel experience except that of a tireless traveller: not a bad training. I once met him, with his chef wife Kay, taking the Thai food course at Bangkok's Oriental Hotel – as a holiday. On his return he quickly found sources of fresh Thai ingredients, and lemon grass and other oriental flavour touches appear on the menu. Paul Henderson has a superb wine list, 400 plus 250 bin ends which must be ordered early so the staff can find them. The list includes, as befits Henderson's American nationality, a lot of Californian wines, and there is an extensive list of digestifs, including ports and malt whiskys.

Paul and Kay opened Gidleigh in 1977. He calls it 'one of the dozen or so most expensive country hotels in Britain', though prices in some of the newer ones are overtaking his. Peace and quiet are guaranteed, with the nearest road 1½ miles away, and the hotel is 700 feet up but set in a basin, with Cawsand Hill rising to 1,800 feet behind the house. In spite of the Tudores-

Gidleigh Park
Chagford, Devon TQ13 8HH
☎ (06473) 2367/8/9
Owners: Paul and Kay Henderson
Co-director, chef: Shaun Hill. Member of Relais et Châteaux.
Price grid A (includes dinner).

Location: Take M4/M3/A30 to Whiddon Down; then go to Chagford (not Gidleigh); in Chagford square, facing Webbers with Lloyds Bank on the right, turn right to Mill Street; after 150 yards fork right downhill to Factory Cross Road; go straight across into Holy Street; follow lane 1½ miles to the end of Gidleigh Park. By rail from London Paddington to Exeter.

que timbering and panelling inside, Gidleigh is nineteenth-century, and was built as a retreat by an Australian shipping magnate. The water gardens are being restored on the banks of the North Teign river, which has a natural swimming pool for the hardy – certainly a good hangover cure after sampling too much from that wine list. The 14 bedrooms are spacious and beautifully kept, with chintzes, china, flowers, plants and lavish use of fabrics, but in most of them the eye is drawn irresistibly to the views over the Teign valley. Four rooms face the forest behind and have compensatingly lower prices. Two rooms in an old chapel have an outside entrance 75 yards from the front door. Like the log fires, Gidleigh's house cats help to give a warm welcome.

The name Bigbury-on-Sea, recalling a fossilized time of sun and sea in the 1920s and 1930s, sets the scene for Burgh Island. The transport from Bigbury beach across a Dijon mustard coloured swathe of sand is by sea tractor. You leave you car on the mainland – the Porters fiercely forbid people to drive across the sand, for reasons all too obvious when the tide turns. The sea tractor that ferries guests across looks like a Victorian bathing machine, mounted on a platform over a high tractor base. It pushes through the swirling waters to the island, and is absolutely necessary since twice a day the 26-acre island and the 26 hotel guests are cut off by the tide. In summer when the tide is in, the tractor runs every thirty minutes

The feeling of isolation from the world and the wonderful sea views from every window create the atmosphere of a murder mystery. It seems a good place for a murder, and indeed Agatha Christie often stayed here and wrote in a little gazebo above the Mermaid Pool, the gale-battered relics of which can still be seen. She wrote *And Then There Were None* here; but *Evil Under the Sun* is actually set on Burgh, and guests can trace the settings – Pixie Cove is 'Bluefin', where Arlene Marshall was strangled – and restore their nerves in the 1920s cocktail bar with an 'Arlene's Revenge', named after the murder victim, and stay in the suite named after the author.

The white, partly castellated, square hotel was designed by Matthew Dawson and built in 1929 by a rich industrialist, Archibald Nettlefold, for his opera singer wife. It was intended as a quiet retreat for entertaining house parties. A few decades earlier, at the end of the nineteenth century, a music-hall singer known as the 'white-eyed Kaffir' had built a wooden hotel on the island; this still exists, and is used

Burgh Island at which guests arrive by sea tractor.

Burgh Island
Bigbury-on-Sea, South Devon TQ7 4AU
☎ (0548) 810514
Owners: Tony and Bea Porter
Price grid A (includes dinner)
Note closed early New Year till mid-March.

Location: M5 to Exeter; M5/ A38 towards Plymouth; 15 miles before Plymouth, with the Woodpecker inn on the left, take exit at Wrangaton Cross; A379 signed to Modbury and follow signs to Bigbury and Bigbury-on-Sea. On arrival phone 810514 from the call box outside main car park by beach at Bigbury-on-Sea, and await collection.
Drive takes about 3½ hours from London. By rail from London Paddington to Plymouth; car collection can be arranged. Helicopter charters available to Burgh Island.

by lifeguards, windsurfers and staff. In the First World war the island was used by the army (as it was in the Second World War); it was sold to Nettlefold in 1927. The glamour set of the day visited: Noël Coward and Lord Mountbatten; the Prince of Wales brought Wallis Simpson to escape the public eye. Eventually after Nettlefold's death the house evolved into the 'smartest hotel west of the Ritz'. These were palmy days, when a maid was stationed outside each room and remained there, heels and back to the wall, all day in case the guests needed anything. There was a resident band, Harry Roy and his Mayfair Four, who were rowed out on summer evenings to a diving platform in the middle of the Mermaid Pool, a natural cliff-enclosed swimming pool which then had sluice gates to keep it full, but is now tidal. After dinner, while Charlie Kunz, Ambrose or Geraldo played, there was dancing in the 36-foot ballroom around a white piano.

Burgh Island fell from its high spot during the war, and by 1985 gales were blowing through broken roofs and through the ballroom. Tony and Bea Porter, fashion experts from London (Bea's sister Barbara Hulanicki created the Biba store in the sixties), saw it on a violent winter day, and sold their house, their prized Daimler and their yacht in order to buy the island. They spent an uncomfortable winter camping in rain-soaked rooms as restoration work got under way. 'We slept in our overcoats in an easterly gale that lasted three weeks.'

The Porters have slaved to recreate the period of the house with Art Deco pieces. Cocktails are served in the stunning stained-glass, Peacock-domed palm court with palms pluming by a fountain. Bea used to buy accessories and lamps as decor for her sister's store, and has now dressed the thirteen suites – all with sitting room and bathroom in pastel shades, giving them a thirties feel, and installed original twenties furniture throughout the hotel. The previous owner had burnt much of the original furniture in a beach fire that lasted two weeks. Morning coffee and afternoon tea are served in the glassed sun lounge with its Lloyd Loom chairs. From the foyer a wide staircase, flanked by jet black glass, leads to the ballroom, where dinner is served to a background of thirties music. The menus offer plenty of seafood; the island has its own summer fisherman, providing mussels, oysters, crab and lobster. A typical daily menu includes dishes like an island fish platter with creamed horseradish and ginger sauce, avocado filled with crab, and tuna topped with a yoghurt and mint dressing; octopus and squid marmalade in olive oil, garlic and fresh chervil is one opener, and

there are usually *moules marinière*, fresh poached Avon salmon, local cheese, Devon ices, sorbets and lots of fruit topped with thick, Devon cream. Vegetarian meals are also available.

Guests can wander over the entire island, find little coves and beaches and swim in the Mermaid Pool, and climb to Agatha Christie's writing spot or to the ruins of the 'huer's hut' (a look-out from which fishermen spotted pilchard shoals and hued, or cried, to colleagues below to set out for the catch). This is on the site of an older chapel, where the ghost of a monk has been seen. Burgh Island was an obvious spot for smugglers. One was called Tom Crocker, who is said to haunt the pub in a friendly way. The pub is the Pilchard Inn, built in 1336 and one of Britain's oldest, where lunch and local beers are served. Croquet, tennis and golf are available over at Bigbury-on-Sea, while the hotel has a games room, with snooker and table tennis, and a small gym. A more sedentary activity is to watch the sea in all its moods, or to observe the birds which nest on the cliffs or in the little bird sanctuary off the island.

Breakfast is taken in the captain's cabin of the 1821 *Ganges*, the last sailing vessel used as flagship of the Royal Navy. Nettlefold bought the cabin in 1930 and stuck it on the front of the house near the Palm Court. There are two slipways for launching dinghies, windsurfers or diving boats, and the Mermaid pool provides a sheltered sun-trap and secret beach for the exclusive use of residents.

Going ashore on the sea tractor, within 30 miles there is Torquay, Widdecombe in the Moor, Buckfast Abbey, and Polperro and nearby on the mainland are little villages of thatched cottages like Thurlestone which can be reached by cliff walks from Bigbury.

The tide covers these sands that join Burgh Island to the Devon shore.

THE COTSWOLDS
Sheep and Shakespeare

The Cotswolds is an endearing area; it is not, however, an easy area to define, and in the imagination of estate agents and tourist organizations it is often made to stretch well beyond the hills which give it its name. It is basically a square, embracing Burford, Chipping Campden, Stroud and Lechlade. One of its characteristics is a friable limestone, ideal for building, that turns golden in the sun. Sidney Smith may have termed the Cotswolds a place of 'stone and sorrows', and it is not the softest of countryside, although in the Middle Ages they used the expression 'as sure as God is in Gloucestershire'. Sheep do well here, at one time big woolly creatures called Cotswold Lions, whose wool was the basis of Elizabethan wealth. Wool merchants built fine houses for their temporal needs, churches and big box tombs for their afterlife. The tombs were big enough to hide poached deer inside, as Shakespeare discovered at an early age when he was fined by the owner of Charlecote Park for poaching in 1588; Shakespeare got his own back in his caricature of the owner as Justice Shallow in Henry IV.

Stratford-on-Avon is strictly just outside the Cotswolds, but is much associated with it; and the Cotswold local has a clear and direct choice of words that has echoes of the Stratford Bard's way of putting things.

The architectural richness, for example in Chipping Campden, where the main street was called by historian G.M. Trevelyan 'the most beautiful village street in England', gives the Cotswolds a wonderful supply of buildings suitable for use as country house hotels. This section ends with four manor houses, all of which mirror the lovely settings and building beauty of the area. Also included are more modern houses, as well as an ancient castle which once protected the border area with Wales on plains once the marshes of the Severn estuary (where Peter Scott has his Slimbridge wild fowl sanctuary).

Ettington Park is at variance with the traditional image of a Cotswold house. It is high Victorian Gothic; with arched church-like windows and high château-inspired roofs and pinnacles, it is akin to its sister hotel Rookery Hall (see page 141). Although Grade I listed and nineteenth-century, the house has a longer pedigree than any of this implies, being, as the brochure puts it, 'the only property in England still in the same ownership as at the time of the Domesday Book'. The building is leased from the Shirley family, who still use the small twelfth-century chapel in the grounds and whose family coat of arms, plus those of 67

Previous pages: Buckland Manor cuddles close to its village church.

Ettington Park Hotel
Alderminster, near Stratford-on-Avon, Warwickshire CV37 8BS
☎ (0789) 740740
Proprietors: Select Country Hotels
Price grid A

Location: 5 miles south of Stratford; 26 miles from Birmingham airport. Take the A34 west from Oxford towards Stratford; after Newbold on Stour (¾ mile) Ettington is on the right of the road and can be glimpsed set back from the A34.

The Victorian conservatory-style entrance to Ettington Park.

families connected to it by marriage, especially decorate the dining room.

Using John Pritchard as architect, antiquarian John Philip Shirley rebuilt the house between 1858 and 1862 in Gothic Revival style and the fourteen bas-reliefs round the exterior record the family history from the time of the Crusades.

Sewallis, son of John Philip, was the founder of the Kennel Club and the last Shirley to live at Ettington. After his time the house was put to a variety of uses, including that of a setting for films. A fire destroyed the main staircase and ceilings and the building continued to deteriorate until 1983, when it became a hotel. In June 1987 Select Country Hotels took over the hotel.

The Victorian charm starts at the entrance, a kind of conservatory, filled with plants and with a floor tiled in a colourful pattern, leading to a darkish panelled hall. The library makes a splendid setting for the hotel bar, with its moulded ceiling, more coats of arms over the towering fireplace, and bookcases filled with fine editions of the classics and Debrett guides; stained-glass windows and deep armchairs heighten the Victorian effect.

The restaurant is a most impressive room with its moulded ceiling and coats of arms inlaid into its panelling. Off the restaurant a chapel with a little stone fireplace and stained-glass windows acts as a small dining room. The menu has a country theme: rabbit terrine with pickled vegetables; globe artichoke and turnip salad; casserole of turbot and mussels baked with carrots and leeks in saffron and dill sauce;

A detail from the Shirley family mottoes at Ettington Park.

braised ox tail on the bone (a rare dish) finished with ox tongue dumpling; Dover sole with lobster sausage studded with truffle; farmhouse cheeses with walnut bread, fruit, and desserts. Chef Patrick McDonald will also prepare vegetarian dishes, and is happy to discuss them with guests in advance.

There is a bizarre story connected with the dining room. Builders in 1856 found a toad alive in a wall cavity, which was reckoned to have been there since the previous building work in 1740. The liberated toad would not eat, and lived in a bottle on the site for a further six months. Its is commemorated in a sculpture on the north exterior wall of the dining room.

The hotel has a courtyard-style swimming pool, with sauna and spa bath, enclosed by glass; in summer the glass walls can be opened out for barbecues and buffets. The 48 bedrooms are in country style with lots of period paintings. Those under the eaves are especially pretty and some bathrooms have whirlpool baths. The Garden suite is very Victorian, with a little fireplace and plenty of bric-à-brac around the twin four-posters. At the top of the house is a long gallery with an arched wooden ceiling; originally designed as a museum for Shirley family treasures, it now acts as a meeting room.

The forty acres of parkland contain a formal Victorian garden, an eighteenth-century folly and a twelfth-century chapel; also there is croquet, tennis, fishing on the Stour and riding from the estate's own stables.

Mallory Court is pretty rather than grand. It is the epitome of chintzy comfort: sofas and tables piled with books and glossy magazines; potpourri, flowering plants, big bays of leaded windows and log fires. The gardens have beautiful lawns, lily ponds, rose garden, tennis and croquet, outdoor pool, and a terrace for summer drinks.

Built as the home of a Midlands car manufacturer, it is as well mannered as its 1920s pedigree. Canapés and drinks are served in deep cushioned chairs in the drawing room or library; then guests go through to the panelled and yellow themed dining room where, under Allan Holland's supervision, head chef Anthony Wright produces *Michelin*-rosetted menus, using herbs and vegetables from the gardens. They nibble home made bread as they await such exquisite dishes as a hot *escalope de foie gras* on toasted brioche with caramelized orange segments; a ravioli of crab, flavoured with ginger; roast young partridge with noodles and grapes and light champagne and orange sauce; or a trio of grilled calves' liver with

Mallory Court
Harbury Lane, Tachbrook Mallory, Leamington Spa, Warwickshire CV33 9QB
☎ (0926) 330214
Owners: Allan Holland and Jeremy Mort. Member of Relais et Châteaux.
Price grid B
Notes unsuitable for children under 12 years. Kennels nearby.

Location: 2 miles south of Leamington Spa. Take B4087 signposted Whitnash. At crossroads, turn left into Harbury Lane; Mallory Court is 500 yards on the right. Stratford 9 miles.

Lily ponds and rose gardens are features of Mallory Court.

raisins, sweetbreads sautéed on creamed leaks, and kidneys with Madeira and mushrooms. Room should be kept for the marvellous desserts: a mousse of chocolate between layers of chocolate squares with orange flavoured *crème anglaise*, or individual apple tarts, flavoured with Calvados.

The same attention to detail has been applied in the bedrooms, where again country colours have been used. The Blenheim suite has a double bathroom, lounge and balcony overlooking the south and rose gardens.

Mallory Court has been a hotel since 1976, and a lot of hard work has been put in to create a spotlessly elegant appearance throughout, from the ten acre gardens to the drapes on the beds. Neither owner comes from a hotel or catering background. Jeremy Mort runs the front of the house, while Allan Holland develops his dishes, helping to make English cooking something to praise not apologize for.

Shakespeare, unlike later writers such as Dickens, Byron, Wordsworth, Wilde and Henry James, did not travel widely enough to have many associations with hotels. But Billesley Manor has perhaps the closest tie, and it is said that *As You Like It* was written in the manor's library. The earliest reference to the manor dates from 705; it was recorded in the Domesday Book, and Shakespeare's maternal grandfather and great-grandfather had trustee property arrangements with the Billesley Manor tenant in the early sixteenth century. William's last surviving descendant, granddaughter Elizabeth Nash (née Hall) married her

Billesley Manor
Billesley, Alcester, Stratford upon Avon, Warwickshire B49 6NE
☎ (0789) 400888
Proprietors: Norfolk Capital Hotels. Member of Prestige.
Price grid B

Location: 3 miles from Stratford. Take A422 towards Alcester from Stratford; after 3 miles turn right and Billesley Manor is on the right.

The new wing at Billesley Manor blends with the old and shelters behind the 1920s yew hedges.

second husband in Billesley church.

In 1905 the owner (who became Lord Sudeley in 1922) built on a new wing and planted the yew hedges that now form thick barricades. In 1912 Henry Tate, of Tate Gallery fame, owned the property and excavated the Barrow. In 1986 the manor was severely damaged by fire, and after renovation it was reopened by Norfolk Capital Hotels in 1987.

The Manor today is set in 11 acres of parkland with the newest wings skilfully blended with the old to give 41 bedrooms. Room 4 has stone-framed windows, oak panelling, a carved wardrobe, gallery, priest's hole and four-poster. The public rooms are a connecting ramble of oak panneling, suits of armour, and log fires. The reception area has a Jacobean-style chest as a desk. Linking the two buildings is an indoor swimming pool and sauna, and outside are tennis courts and lawns used for boules and croquet.

The owners of Langley stress that their house is not a hotel – 'it's just a family home'. Set airily high on a typical Cotswold ridge just outside Winchcombe, it is a close neighbour of Sudeley Castle, where Katherine Parr, widow of Henry VIII, lived with Lady Jane Grey, and where Katherine's tomb can be seen. Langley is full of character and comfort. Outside there is a south-facing patio, and seven acres of well-stocked terraced garden, which seem to be in flower through the seasons with snowdrops, acconites, lavender hedges, wisteria, dahlias and clematis climbing over a pergola. The house has a paddock, a

Langley House's garden provides a seasonal change of colour and plenty of wild birds.

Langley Country House
Winchcombe,
Gloucestershire GL54 5AB
☎ (0242) 603959
Owners: Mr and Mrs R.T. Herring. Members of Wolsey Lodge.
Price grid C

Location: 7 miles north of Cheltenham towards Stratford and Winchcombe; go through Prestbury to the top of Cleeve Hill, descend for half a mile, and take the unmarked turning on the left opposite the sign 'Stratford/ Cheltenham'; follow the lane for about half a mile, and Langley's wide gravel driveway is on the left. Coming from Winchcombe, turn right at Corner Cupboard Inn into Langley Road.

water garden and a tennis court; and there is a good chance of seeing woodpeckers, jays and tame sparrow-hawks. There are walks to Cleeve Hill, where there is a public golf course offering marvellous views over the Vale of Evesham to the Malverns and, on a clear day, the Welsh hills.

Inside there is a large lounge along the whole length of the house, filled with paintings and offering views out to the steep flanks of Cleeve Hill. There is a licensed bar, with leaded windows. A maximum of six visitors can be accommodated. The house was rebuilt at the turn of the century by Lady Duran, but the original house dates back to the seventeenth century, with beautiful stone mullions with leaded windows. There is an indoor swimming pool. The Herrings, who run a quality fashion store and shoe shop in Cheltenham (hence the unusual shoe fashion prints lining the bedroom corridor), mastermind dinners which are a procession of traditional dishes: smoked salmon, home-made soups, seafood, chicken breast with Madeira sauce, vegetables from the garden, home-made sorbets and ice-creams. Guests are asked whether they prefer to stay in for dinner, and advice is freely given on nearby restaurants. Afternoon tea is served with home-made preserves, scones, cakes and shortbread.

Tony Jacklin, the golfer, owned Langley during the 1970s, and it was he who put in the swimming pool and carried out much of the modernization. All the four bedrooms are centrally heated and have their own bathrooms, two with brass fittings and original toilets. The beds have electric blankets, and there are direct dial phones with print-out billing, televisions and tea-making facilities. Sherry, chocolates, fresh fruit and magazines are also provided. Style ranges from a locally made four-poster to pine country furniture.

The Greenway, set back from the main road, is a three-storey, gabled and creeper-clad Cotswold house backing on to farmland rising to wooded hills. The flag-stoned entrance hall has heavy oak doors, and high-backed settees around a big log fire. Greenway's name comes from a pre-Roman path running beside the hotel. A 'greenway' was a drovers' road, a safe walk way. This one goes up into the hills behind the hotel, and leads to Long Barrow, an early burial site, and the remains of a pre-Iron Age fort.

Early owners were sixteenth-century woollen traders, one of whom, William Lawrence, built the house in 1584. The family continued living there until 1854, and it became a hotel in 1947.

When a seventeenth-century Lawrence tragically lost both wife and heir, he made a plan to turn the entire grounds into a memorial to them. His original intention was to include a mount flanked by alms houses and topped with a chapel containing the dear departed's remains. This was never built, but near the house a series of sunken gardens were planted, symbolizing the successive ages of man.

The Greenway's interior is far from mournful. The big drawing room is full of comfortable, flowery sofas and big windows looking on to the lawns. The Gothic conservatory-style dining

The Greenway
Shurdington, Cheltenham, Gloucestershire GL51 5UG
☎ (0242) 862352
Managing Director: Tony Elliott. Member of Pride of Britain.
Price grid A
Notes no children under 7 years; no pets.

Location: On A46 Cheltenham/Stroud road 2½ miles from Cheltenham and 2 miles from Exit 11 of the M5. By rail from London Paddington to Cheltenham. Helicopter pad.

The Greenway's sheltered rear terrace forms the setting for alfresco summer meals.

room opens on to a paved area around a pond.

Big portraits line the stairs leading up to the bedrooms, most of which are spacious and have views over the grounds. Ten rooms are in the main house, eight in the converted coach-house. Characteristic decor notes are floral fabrics, bird tiles around fireplaces, chinoiserie lamps, dressing areas and half-tester beds.

The Greenway is well sited for touring or shopping in Cheltenham, and the hotel has plenty of tour sheet suggestions, which incude local pubs, Roman villas to visit and local walks from behind the hotel.

To restore the inner man on the return, seasonal menus are planned by Tony Robson-Burrell. In Spring, a clear soup of chicken and smoked goose is garnished with wild mushroom ravioli; Dublin Bay prawns are served with vegetable julienne with a spicey peanut sauce, and roast breast of Gressingham duck with spring cabbage and spinach galette and redcur-rant-flavoured sauce. The pudding menu in-cludes warm soup of seasonal fruits; glazed sliced fruit plate with Tia Maria sabayon; and *millefeuille* of Belgian chocolate with fresh pineapple cream and coffee-bean sauce.

T he only surviving Tudor castle/palace, Thornbury is a castle in the true sense; built when a man needed a solid house to protect himself. This did not save its creator, the third Duke of Buckingham, who began to build it in 1510, having obtained permission from Henry VIII to castellate a common manor house. In 1521 he was convicted of treason and executed on Tower Hill. His lands were confis-cated, and the castle appropriated by Henry VIII, who in 1535 stayed at Thornbury with Ann Boleyn. Mary Tudor later lived there for some time, but returned the castle to the Buckingham family in 1554.

Two centuries of neglect have left ruined wings, in part of which new suites have recently been constructed. Today the castle lies tran-quilly beside the tall parish church tower, its grey-walled gardens and vineyard approached through an imposing gateway. The vineyard was planted by Kenneth Bell, who with his Elizabeth restaurant in Oxford was responsible for a renaissance in English catering cookery. The vineyard grapes now go to the Three Choirs company to be turned into Thornbury label wines which can be bought at the castle. Bell bought Thornbury in 1966 for £26,000 and later put in bathrooms for the guest bedrooms, tunnelling through walls a yard thick and removing 15 tons of rubble per bathroom. When Bell bought Thornbury it was big enough to have one wing on the Oldbury telephone

Thornbury Castle
Thornbury, Bristol
BS12 1HH
☎ (0454) 418511
Owners: Maurice and Carol Taylor. Member of Pride of Britain.
Price grid A
Notes Open at Christmas for residents only. Closed for ten days in January. No children under 12 years. No pets.

Location: Leave M4 at exit 20 and take A38 north and B4461 signed to Thornbury; in Thornbury continue downhill to the northern edge of the village; the castle lodge and gates are beside the parish church. By rail from London Paddington to Bristol Parkway. Helicopter pad.

exchange and another on the Thornbury exchange.

In the 18 bedchambers one can sleep on a bed tented like a pink brocade palanquin, sweep through stone-framed doors, and swing wooden iron-hinged shutters over the oriel windows. Tudor windows still exist in the octagonal tower room, and the towering window sweep above the drawing room has 720 panes of curved glass. A single room in one of the turrets was once the Buckingham jewel chamber.

Stone corridors waft guests down to big sitting rooms; the dining room is hung with tapestries and has a huge open fire. Wines are kept in the dungeons. The food prepared by chef Colin Hingston is English with French influences, but many of the Kenneth Bell favourites have been kept, notably chicken breast in Pernod, hot butterscotch pudding, and Thornbury treacle tart. Athol Brose and lemon syllabub are other old desserts that Henry VIII would have liked, along with sirloin, the meat he knighted, served at the traditional Sunday lunch, or the substantiation of dishes like venison and port pie. A raspberry sorbet is served on a meringue knot in the shape of the Stafford knot which adorns the castle's outside walls, its shape said to be for the purpose of hanging three people.

In the grounds the walled gardens provide a sheltered place to sit, and one can see the excavations of the heraldic tiled floor of the old manor's banqueting hall, dated 1500. To get the best view of the castle's setting and design one can take a trip with the Bristol Balloon Company. Special tours are arranged for guests by Stand and Stare Tours in South Wales, a company set up by redundant steel workers.

Thornbury Castle is splendidly regal; Henry VIII and Mary Tudor stayed here.

Thanks to the motorways, people can and do zip down to Calcot for Sunday lunch from London, Cardiff and the Midlands. The *Michelin*-starred food is as English as the whole family-run complex. Calcot is ideally set for exploring the Cotswolds, Bath and Cheltenham. Westonbirt arboretum is 10 minutes away, one of Britain's top attractions for tree enthusiasts, particularly in autumn for the scarlets and golds. Malmesbury Abbey is 15 minutes away, and the Cotswold Way nearby. Calcot helps with pub information and picnic hampers. Gatcombe is 15 minutes away for the August horse trials and there is a golf course nearby. The hotel grounds include a small arboretum, and gardens which provide flowers for the rooms and herbs for the kitchen; and clay pigeon shooting is available.

Brian and Barbara Ball are such amiable hosts, and Calcot so appealing with its shel-

Calcot Manor
near Tetbury,
Gloucestershire GL8 8YJ
☎ (066 689) 391
Owners: Brian and Barbara Ball. Member of Pride of Britain.
Price grid B
Note No children under 12 years.

Location: Leave M4 at exit 18; take A46 north towards Cheltenham, then A4135 right towards Tetbury; Calcot is on the left near the turn-off. Tetbury 3 miles.

tered gardens and swimming pool, that many guests choose to stay in and unwind. Calcot is not grand; until 1983, when the Balls bought it and converted it to a hotel, it was known as Calcot Farm. But the building dates back to the fifteenth-century, and across the courtyard is the second oldest Tythe barn in England. The former stables are now suites, in which the use of light floral fabrics against the solid timbers creates a delightful effect. There are also holiday cottages in a seventeenth-century granary barn across the croquet lawn.

The future of the Tythe barn has not been decided, although the Balls are considering turning it into some kind of hall for music recitals. The barn was built by Cistercian monks from nearby Kingswood Abbey in the fourteenth century. Built in Cotswold stone, it measures 130 by 37 feet. The entrance of the barn is floodlit at night, and on New Year's Eve a piper appears from the barn at midnight.

The public rooms have a relaxed farmhouse atmosphere, with lots of books, magazines and flowers, and comfortable chairs to sink into by the fires. The Balls are not just gifted amateurs, however. Brian is a Swiss-trained hotelier and for 25 years was catering adviser to BP in London. His son Richard has trained in London, Paris and Oxford. Their chef, Ramon Farthing, trained in Colchester and worked at the Maison Talbooth (see page 119), and at the Castle Hotel in Taunton. He came to Calcot in 1986 and, though he has never worked outside England, gained a *Michelin* star in nine months. The first thing is flavour, he says – 'then presentation from there'. He smokes his own meat, fish comes from Brixham, and he offers a choice in *table d'hôte* selections. Afternoon tea by the fire or in the garden includes home-made scones, ginger cake and shortbread (also made for the bedrooms). Canapés and chocolates to go with the coffee afterwards are made fresh each evening. Farthing is keen to promote British produce. Only British and Irish cheeses are served. Calcot's English Luncheon is full of country warmth; hot mushroom and mustard soup, garnished with chives; hot tartlet of smoked cheese; smoked loin of English veal with cabbage and bacon stuffing, light artichoke mousse and dark veal sauce flavoured with truffle essence (sauce spoons are provided); smooth plum sorbet in light butter pastry with cream vanilla sauce, or warm tartlet of Bramley apple baked on an almond sponge with fresh apple sauce and Calvados and sultana ice-cream. A chef's selection of six popular light courses can be served as a surprise dinner for one to four people.

The breakfast is real country house magnificence; hot home-made mueslis, 'main' courses of finnan haddock and poached egg, local grilled trout and green herbs and lemon, grilled bacon, Gloucester sausage, tomato and mushroom, cold honey roast ham and fresh farm eggs, all in the room price. Richard Ball masterminds the wine list, which is mostly French but also includes wines from Chile, Australia, California and, more locally, Three Choirs. Helpful taste notes are appended and there is a good choice of half-bottles.

Between meals a rest in one's room is probably indicated. Barbara Ball has put a great deal of thought into her choice of fabrics and little aids to travel enjoyment (right down to the generous supplies of toiletries in the ladies' room with its soft pink and grey decor). On the landing at the top of the carved staircase, the work of local craftsmen, the bowl of fruit from which guests can help themselves is another thoughtful touch. The 13 bedrooms echo aspects of the region; the Chiltern room, for example, has 'hedgerow' wallpaper, matching fabrics and bramble-patterned bathroom tiles, while the Cotswold room has hand-crafted mirrors and floral chintzes. The Master room has a canopied and draped four-poster and a whirlpool bath. Soft pastel shades are used in most rooms, and all rooms have settees and two armchairs for snoozing or reading the books provided. Brian Ball says, 'We welcome every guest ourselves as they arrive at Calcot. We treat them all as our private guests in our own home and are somewhat surprised when they ask for a bill.'

Calcot Manor is a welcoming family house noted for its food and comfort.

The entrance to Buckland Manor.

Near the well-kept, green-verged village of Broadway, that gave its name to that theatre street in New York, lies Buckland Manor in its archetypal Cotswold setting. The thirteenth-century manor nestles close to the church. At the back, its ten acres of garden, which include a tennis court, putting green, croquet lawn and heated pool, climb a sheltered hillside, crossed by streams which feed its water gardens. The only somewhat incongruous note is struck by the Highland cattle and Jacob sheep grazing by the entrance.

The site of Buckland Manor house was first mentioned in the seventh century, when its land was given by the Saxon king of Mercia to Eadburgha, abbess of Gloucester. Later, after the dissolution of the monasteries, the house passed to the Gresham family, lord mayors of London, financiers and philanthropists and after whom London's Gresham Street is named. The manor remained in private hands until bought by the Bermans in 1981.

On arrival, greeting is proferred by Charlie – not a porter, but the Bermans' sheep-dog. Inside, the rooms are heavily panelled, with stone-flagged floors, arched doorways, beamed ceilings, log fire, oak furniture and mullioned windows. The dining room, candle-lit at night, looks out on the back gardens. Chef Martyn Pearn, previously at the Chelsea Room and the Connaught in London and La Réserve in Bordeaux, finds that his lunches are in no less demand here, with many people touring in the area. Elaborate calligraphy and liberal use of French characterize the menu, on which the main courses tend to include local salmon, guinea fowl and lamb.

Four of the eleven bedrooms have 'coal' gas fires, and two have four-posters. Some of the rooms have views of the hills, on top of which runs the Cotswold Way. The Summer room is decorated in yellow and has hand-made Victorian tiles; the Floral suite is the largest of the twin-bedded rooms, and has a massive bathroom. There are also three bedrooms on the ground floor, including the Abbot's room, next to the thirteenth-century church.

Charingworth is set on a shelf in the hillside, which, as you approach through its 54 acres of grazing land, gradually lifts the manor into view: a classic Cotswold stone building with gables and tall chimneys, against a background of trees and formal gardens studded with those stone mushrooms on which coffins were rested on their way to country churchyards.

Charingworth was recorded in the Domesday Book, but the present building dates from

Buckland Manor
Buckland, nr Broadway,
Worcester, Gloucestershire
WR12 7LY
☎ (0386) 852626
Owners: Barry and Adrienne Berman
Price grid A
Note: Closed for 3½ weeks from mid-January.

Location: Take the A44 to Broadway; turn left on A46/B4632 towards Cheltenham; just after leaving Broadway is Buckland village; the Manor is on the right next to the church.

early Tudor times, and the library has chevron-painted beams showing original decorations painted in about 1316. The first owner, according to the Domesday Book, was Ralph de Tosyn, 'who held with Charingworth 3 ploughs, 13 villages, and 1 riding man, with 6 ploughs, 9 slaves male and female. The value was £8, now £6'. It cost somewhat more in January 1987, when the Gregory family bought it from the Creswell family. As Darryl Gregory puts it, 'It was set to tumble. Domestic insurance and rates being so high, it had to become a hotel.'

Helped by their mother's decorative flair, the brothers have completed restoration of the manor with fabrics and decoration in sympathy with the partly Jacobean additions; for example, stencilwork round the library fire. The curtains have the look of tapestry, and go well with the low ceilings and smallish windows. There are crewel-work curtains, cross-stitch carpets, and bare, natural stone around the fireplaces. The library beams have been authenticated by the British Museum as painted in owner Edward Burnell's time on original ship's timber. The sitting rooms opening off the hall are small and intimate, particularly the one by the front door.

More rooms are being added in stables linked with the manor by a glass-covered gallery. Many of the bedrooms are named after previous owners; an exception to this rule is 'T.S. Eliot'; the poet was a regular house guest in the 1930s, and used to write here. His twin-bedded room is up in the roof space. The whole building has interesting nooks and crannies and sudden changes of level: bathroom or bedroom may be up a few steps. The bathrooms have brass taps, old-style baths and Italian hand-made tiles. 'Edward Burnell' has a wooden-topped four-poster with a quilt which

Charingworth Manor
near Chipping Campden, Gloucestershire GL55 6NS
☎ (038 678) 555
Owners: Nigel and Darryl Gregory
Price grid B
Note Closed mid-January to mid-February. No children under 12; dogs by arrangement.

Location: take the A34 from Oxford to Shipston on Stour; turn left on to the B4035 and cross the A429; Charingworth is signed on the right soon after the crossroads. Chipping Campden 3 miles; Stratford 10 miles.
By rail from London Paddington to Moreton in the Marsh, 6 miles. Car collection can be arranged.

Charingworth Manor is set on a terraced hill near Chipping Camden.

apparently took three hundred hours to make; the linen fold panelling on the cupboards came from Lloyd George's library. Televisions are tucked away in cabinets, and small safes are set under the window seats.

The dining room, named after John Grevill, is a long narrow area, divided into sections, which lends intimacy to the 55 seats. The upper walls are 'ragged and dragged' and the specially made dining chairs (patented by the Gregorys) are large and comfortable, with padded arms. When the position of chef was advertised, over three hundred applications were received; Melvin Rumbolds won after a three-day 'cook-off'. With his entirely British staff he produces Charingworth Fayre, a three-course menu which might feature calves' liver pudding with peppers and beetroot and winter vegetable parcels; or breast of wood pigeon with lambs' tongue mousse, soft green peppercorns and piquant red claret sauce. One can go down through a trap door to visit the cellars, where tastings are occasionally held and where diners can select a wine.

The 0451 phone code stands for the Cotswold exchange, and Lower Slaughter and its manor could hardly have a more attractive and characteristically Cotswold setting. The village meanders along the River Eye with little greens, stone-built houses and cottages set beside its banks. The name of this peaceful spot does not commemorate some awful blood-letting, but is supposed to be a corruption of the name of a Norman knight, Philipe de Sloitre, who was given land in the area by William I.

The manor, recently renovated and restored, was once the home of the High Sheriff of Gloucestershire and goes back over a thousand years. On the site was a former convent with two-storey dovecot said to have kept the nuns supplied with food. Much of the present building dates from the seventeenth-century, when the west wing was added; the big stone fireplace is dated 1658. In 1655 the owner contracted Valentine Strong to build a house for £200. Valentine Strong was an important stone-mason; his son Thomas was the principal contractor employed by Wren to build St Paul's Cathedral. The blue peach drawing room has a contemporary ceiling of medallions of fruit flowers, birds and angelic female figures.

The house has 16 double and 3 single rooms named for girls. A decanter of sherry, fruit and books are placed in each room which are decorated in floral chintzes. There is an indoor pool, with sauna and solarium.

Lower Slaughter Manor
Lower Slaughter,
Gloucestershire GL54 2HP
☎ (0451) 20456
Owners: Premier Hotels
General Manager: Peter Hawkes.
Price grid B
Note No children under 8 years. No pets; kennels can be arranged.

Location: Take the M40 from London; continue on the A40 past Oxford; turn right on to the A429 Bourton on the Water (Stow Road); after Bourton turn left to Lower Slaughter; the manor is in the village centre next to the church.

The menu offers five choices for each course (plus six desserts) including a different home-made soup each day, a layered terrine of salmon and sole, roast pigeon with raspberry vinegar and bitter chocolate, and home-made cinnamon ice-cream. The hotel grows its own herbs and vegetables; there are free-range eggs, home-made preserves, and honey which comes from Cotswold bees. Cheese is served as an extra course, and the cheese list offers a choice of ten, all British, with careful explanations. It includes Shropshire Blue, Single Gloucester, Cerney goats from the Cotswolds, Cotherstone, a rare Teesdale cheese now made only in one farmhouse, St Killian, Lanark Blue, Wedmore and Colston Bassett Stilton.

The wine list is a well-presented booklet with a good index at the front, easy to follow and much more convenient than those large folded lists which tend to blot out the light from the table lamp. There are tasting notes alongside the red burgundies, which, like the red Bordeaux, are divided into conventional wines and classified growths of older vintage. Apart from European wines, Australian, Californian and South African wines are listed.

The manor has a croquet lawn, a tennis court and its own trout fishing from the banks of the River Eye. There is plenty to see and do within a few miles. The Cotswold Farm Park run by Joe Henson at Guiting Power shows off the traditional farm animals and rare breeds like the Cotswold Lion sheep and Gloucester Old Spot pigs. A weekend of village-hopping could include Bourton on the Water, Stow on the Wold, Lower Swell, Hidcote, Bibury and the larger Chipping Norton.

Lower Slaughter Manor is built in golden Cotswold stone.

EAST ANGLIA
AND THE MIDLANDS

A Feudal Feeling

There is no lack of manor houses and substantial farmhouses in East Anglia and the Midlands, but a smaller proportion of them contain hotels than in more southern and western areas of England. This is partly because houses here change hands less frequently; partly because people tend to rush through the Midlands on their way north, while in East Anglia, which tends to attract weekenders and boating people, there is less demand for hotel accommodation. In the hunting counties of the Midlands traditional landowners have retained an almost feudal hold, though Stapleford Park, itself once a vast hunting retreat, is now a hotel.

East Anglia is at its most relaxing out of season, such is the popularity of the Broads in high summer. Its flatter countryside concentrates the attention on its buildings, particularly its church spires built, as in the Cotswolds, with wool merchants' money. Lavenham, Long Melford and Thaxsted are good examples. Windmills are another skyline feature, as at Saxted, and the East Anglia tourist board issues a list of those which can be visited. Vegetables and herbs, widely grown in the area as well as flowers, enhance hotel tables.

The East Anglian coast produces some of England's best seafood: sprats, eels, kippers, Yarmouth bloaters, Colchester oysters, crabs from Cromer, while the Butley Orford oysterage is famed. Norfolk is noted for its turkeys, once sent to London's markets with their feet shod with protective 'shoes'. A variety of smoked meats comes from Kersey and Peasenhall. Preserves are made commercially in Cambridgeshire and Essex.

West Norfolk, the area around King's Lynn, famous for its fish market, is less well known; while inland from Hunstanton, the big beach resort, backed by forest and heathland, there are charming red-brick villages each indicated by an elaborately carved sign along the road. Lavender is grown here and can be seen being processed at Caley Mill, near Heacham. Craftsmen make a wide range of souvenirs from candles to crystal. The coast also has several nature reserves; the one at Holme Next the Sea is the largest in the country. Southern East Anglia, in spite of motorway access, has not changed too substantially, and Gerald Milsom at the Maison Talbooth can point to sweeps of countryside that appear much as they did to John Constable when he put them on canvas. Constable was a local miller's son, and Gainsborough was also from East Anglia, born in Ipswich. The Romans built colonies in East Anglia and introduced pheasants to Britain – still a staple food here. Later, the Danes

Previous pages: New Hall is reputed to be the oldest, moated house in England.

invaded the area, their presence now commemorated in place names ending in 'toft' or 'thwaite'. Weavers persecuted on the Continent settled here; hence the Flemish-style buildings like Westerfield Hall near Ipswich.

The Birmingham suburbs are an unlikely setting for what is reputed to be the oldest moated manor house in England. Begun in 1200, New Hall belies its title and forms a tranquil oasis surrounded by its lily-filled water. A boat is needed to ferry a mowing machine across the moat to cut the grass of the inner garden. The gardens and parkland have yew tree walks, a summer arbour, an avenue of Christmas trees planted out by previous owners, as well as archery and croquet.

A grandson of Lady Godiva owned the land before the Norman Conquest, but the moat was not dug until 1340 when the building was put up; most of its grey and white masonry still remains. A wing and Great Chamber were added for the visit of Henry VIII. Henry was nearly harmed by a wild boar in the park, happily shot just in time by a young girl. Henry presented her with a Tudor rose, which since then has been the emblem of Sutton Coldfield, the girl's home village.

In 1590, under Henry Sacheverell the hall was largely rebuilt. His son was a Cavalier and it is said that Charles II spent a night here during his escape from England. The estate's ghost, a bodiless head (a reversal of most), dates from the Jacobite rebellion period. The man was decapitated by the Duke of Cumberland's men who thought he might be a Jacobite sympathiser as they marched north against Bonnie Prince Charlie in 1746, and his head was thrown into an oak tree. When the tree was felled in 1827, the skull rolled out, and since then the ghost's head has been roaming to discover the spot where his body was buried.

New Hall became a school in the late nineteenth century, and the boys' pastime seems to have been throwing ink wells into the moat, judging by the number found when it was cleaned out. Later the hall was bought by Alfred Owen, a Midland industrialist active in developing the motor car – he created the pressed steel chassis in 1896 – as well as cycles and aeroplanes. He collected Joseph Kronheim Victorian prints, and put them in a vault for later framing. After his death in 1929 the prints lay forgotten till 1981. Perfectly preserved, they were bought back for the hotel at a Christie's sale in 1987 and provide the inspiration for the menu designs. High maintenance costs forced a recent owner to sell the estate in 1985, since when Thistle Hotels have extended rather than

New Hall
Walmley Road, Sutton Coldfield, Warwickshire B76 8QX
☎ (021 378) 2442
Proprietors: Thistle Hotels
General Managers: Ian and Caroline Parkes
Price grid B
Note Not suitable for children under 8 years.

Location: 7 miles from the centre of Birmingham; take Exit 5 off the M6 going north (6 if southbound), or from the centre of Birmingham the A38 expressway. New Hall is on the B4148 on north-west side of Walmley on edge of Sutton Coldfield. Car collection from airport and station can be arranged. Helicopter pad.

altered it, adding a new wing of 53 rooms.

After a £4 million refurbishment the hotel opened in May 1988. Although owned by a chain, it has been left as an individual country house hotel, the flagship of the group, with Ian and Caroline Parkes acting as resident managers and hosts. Caroline is much involved in room decoration and housekeeping, and their Labrador Rupert extends their welcome to guests when not diving into the moat. Caroline describes the house's interior with its different periods of alterations as 'a walk through time'. The inner hall looks out on the water, which actually runs under the room. Heraldic devices of owning families decorate the staircase, and on the first floor there are more coats of arms on the ceiling timbers of the Red Landing which leads to the Great Chamber, where wedding receptions are now held. Built around 1542 and enlarged in the late sixteenth century, it has an oak floor, panelled walls and a ribbed ceiling with mouldings of grapes, foliage, faces and scrolls. The windows have original sixteenth-century glass, leaded in a geometrical pattern and later incised with Latin quotations on the subject of love, in 1689.

The bedrooms, tended by housemaids in frilled Victorian-style pinafores, are named after lily varieties found in the moat. 'Clarissa' has a blue and white theme and contains a four-poster and Chinese lamps. One room has a raised corner bath in a tiny alcove prettied with Victorian prints hung on bows and a strawberry-patterned wallpaper. 'Sirius' is a beamed attic room with elephant-legged table and a wardrobe in the style of a crusader tent. 'Amabilis' is a single room with a small corner fireplace which is lit in winter. 'Alba' in the thirteenth-century wing has another corner fireplace and views of the moat. It is opposite 'Candida', a low-ceilinged room with beams and a raised sitting area in the window overlooking the moat.

Lilies are gathered for the restaurant tables, and the walled garden supplies herbs and flowers for the hall. Stained glass and family crests decorate the thirteenth-century dining room and the small, adjoining oak room, hung with tapestries, which is to become the no smoking area. Chef Allan Garth, formerly at Gravetye, and 'sous chef' Nigel Hitches from Greywalls prepare all the pastry and baked goods in the hotel, and smoke their own trout, salmon and venison.

In spite of its proximity to the hub of motorways, Grafton Manor retains a rural feel (it would be more rural, since the addition of a third motorway lane, if the

Grafton Manor was mortgaged by the owner, the Earl of Shrewsbury, to finance William and Mary's claim to the throne.

Morrises were allowed to carry out the planting of a screen of trees in their six acres). There is coarse fishing in a two-acre lake, a paddock for family horses, and croquet on the lawn. A 1¼-acre formal herb garden, one of the largest in the UK, has been created by John Morris at the back of the house. Its 144 herb beds, each three yards square, are seen to best effect from upper windows. At its centre is an early nineteenth-century urn and radiating out from it are antique roses, the petals of which are mixed with herbs to make the potpourri for the manor.

The Morris family are a self-sufficient brood. John Morris originally perceived Grafton as a restaurant for his wife and their daughter though members of the family had lived there for some time. Cut off by the snow in 1982, they used the enforced lay-off to convert the bedrooms themselves and since then have created a total of nine. Their first guest turned out to be a *Michelin* inspector.

The manor was built in 1567 by the Earl of Shrewsbury, who placed his motto 'prêt d'accomplier' over his arms on the fireplace in the first floor bar/sittingroom – a tag that could apply equally well to the present owner. The Shrewsburys were a leading Catholic family, and they and their house were involved in dramatic episodes of history such as the Gunpowder Plot (through which they lost arms and furniture, taken and sold by the state). Grafton acted as refuge for Catholic priests, and the Grafton priest was the last in Worcestershire to be put to death for his faith in 1679. In Charles II's reign the Earl of Shrewsbury took his place at court again. However, his wife fell in love with the Duke of Buckingham, who killed

Grafton Manor
Grafton Lane, Bromsgrove, Worcestershire B61 7HA
☎ (0527) 579007
Owners: The Morris family. Members of Pride of Britain.
Price grid B
Notes No children under 7 years; no pets.

Location: Turn off M5 at Exit 4 (northbound) or Exit 5 (southbound); then after passing through Bromsgrove to 1 mile south off B4090 Worcester road, then turn down Grafton Lane; the manor is at the end.
By rail from London Euston to New Street, Birmingham or Birmingham International. Direct link to Birmingham airport and National Exhibition Centre by M42.

Shrewsbury in a duel (watched by his wife, disguised as a page). His son Charles helped remove James II from the throne and escorted in William and Mary. Grafton was used as a meeting place for the conspirators and was mortgaged to finance William and Mary's arrival. He then became Secretary of State and Lord Treasurer under Queen Anne.

Grafton's rooms are comfortable, with thoughtful extras, and the family keep a close eye on everything. Stephen runs the front of house with his mother, while the twins, Nicola and Simon are joint chefs. They buy fish from Birmingham and vegetables from Evesham, collect wild strawberries to make jam, and use sorrel, wild angelica and grapes from the garden to help vary the menu every day. One of their most popular puddings is whisky-steamed pudding. Their flavourings are adventurous: pike mousse with mint and sage sauce; roast baby duck with kumquat and Van der Hum sauce; boned sardines stuffed with cheese and herb paté, grilled and served with garden salad; squid provençal; salad of avocado pear with sweet pickled herring and horseradish cream; lambs' hearts roasted and stuffed with cheese and onion with Madeira sauce; grouse pudding with cranberry and juniper berry sauce. A vegetarian menu is available on request.

Stapleford Park has one of the country's finest stable blocks built by Lord John Gretton in the last century.

Melton Mowbray is hunt country and has a hunt cake (served with the stirrup cup) named after it, and huntsmen whooping it up there are said to have originated the phrase 'painting the town red'. Edward Prince of Wales wanted to buy Staple-

The clocktower and cloisters at Stapleford Park.

ford Park, but Queen Victoria forbade it, fearing his morals would be corrupted by the Leicester hunting society. American owner Bob Payton, who first saw the house from horseback, has spent £4½ million on it.

The house dates back to the sixteenth century, but has seventeenth- and nineteenth-century additions. Until the 1850s it was the seat of the Earls of Harborough, descendants of William I. At the end of the nineteenth century Lord John Gretton bought it as a country retreat and hunting lodge and installed a double-storey ballroom. He built a magnificent stable block, considered one of the country's finest; Payton is restoring it to its original purpose and will eventually offer riding facilities from the 55-acre park.

Payton's businesses include the Chicago Pizza Pie Factory, Chicago Meat Packers restaurants and Henry J. Bean's bar and grills. But Payton's original qualification and career were in advertising and he has drawn on this flair in establishing Stapleford, while using Chewton Glen as a role model. He has shocked many purists, and not just with his startling room decor. 'You can't put a minigolf course in a Victorian walled garden,' said his advisers – but he did, and it fits in well.

The rooms are indeed unusual, but nothing compared to some of the eccentric extravaganzas of the past perpetuated by English owners, and the English are supposed to treasure an eccentric. Payton had the bright idea of getting top designers and English companies each to design one of the 30 existing rooms (which will eventually rise to fifty). Liberty, Tiffany and Co and Lindka Cierach, who designed Fergie's wedding gown and here uses taffetas, laces and moires, have all done rooms. Crabtree and Evelyn's room is a boudoir of floral chintz with walls crammed with botanical prints and a bathroom full of their products and *trompe l'œil* scenes over the bath. Wedgwood's Jasper room has a four-poster, and a portrait of Josiah Wedgwood gazing down; blue and white shades from the Jasper ware are used with pale blue wallpaper hand-blocked with Greek figures and Waterford (who own the Wedgwood company) lamps and chandelier. The rooms designed by Nina Campbell and Jane Churchill are less dramatic. Nina Campbell has used airy *toile de Jouey* for the ceiling, walls and curtains of a gallery bedroom in a three-level suite made out of the old ballroom space, and paisley and red for a 'gentleman's library' sitting room.

Payton has put much thought into the bathrooms with big tubs, mahogany surrounds, nickel taps, and basins set at a special and more comfortable height. The most striking idea is in

Stapleford Park
near Melton Mowbray, Leicestershire LE14 2EF
☎ (057 284) 522
Owners: Bob and Wendy Payton. Members of Prestige.
Price grid A
Notes No children under 10 years. Kennels and stables in the grounds; dogs, cats and horses looked after.

Location: Take the A1 from the south at Colsterworth roundabout, take the B676 towards Melton Mowbray; follow the B676 for 9 miles; 1 mile past village of Saxby turn left for Stapleford.

the Max Pike room, where the free-standing bath is placed in the bedroom window alcove, so that you can see the television or the parkland while you soak.

The Turnbull and Asser room uses shirt material for wall coverings, silk and tweed for chair upholstery, while the curtains are in smoking jacket velour trimmed with silk and held back with hand-made silk ties. Shirt illustrations by current designers are hung on the walls with moire silk trouser braces. I stayed in 'Lady Gretton', which has a warm, hunting lodge atmosphere, with its dark green walls, big green and red tartan bedhead and day sofa. The television is discreetly concealed in a cabinet but has 24-hour satellite channels. The tartan is a variation of Payton's 'house tartan', which is also used in the sweaters of the young men who act as receptionists and hall porters. The staff of fifty, young and local, may be informal but they are also friendly and help-ful, which does much to soften the formality of the decor and helps to make Stapleford a happier place.

The public rooms are huge and full of large feet-up sofas and conversation areas. Large bronze statues of ballet dancers are set around the rooms. The *trompe l'œil* decoration round the gallery of the main staircase includes a portrait of Wendy's giant schnauzer dog peering down. The real-life Gunther helps greet guests wearing a bandana round his neck and is very happy to share their tea-time cookies. The library with its own, small bar is a cosy after-dinner spot.

Payton is employing chefs supplied by Richard Shepherd of Langan's. Meals are served in a stately room with Grinling Gibbons carvings and a rather hushed air, which Payton is anxious to dissipate. Food mixes in trans-atlantic ideas; guinea fowl comes with chili hash browns. And when you finally go to bed, a house Teddy Bear waits on the pillow, if you so request, along with a tin of Wendy's chocolate chip cookies, to comfort you among the tartans and shirtings.

Breakfast is taken in the old kitchen with its vaulted ceiling and attractive home-made pots of preserves in a venerable fireplace alcove. The choice of curried haddock, waffles with syrup, pancakes, blueberry muffins or crois-sants blends breakfast ideas from both sides of the Atlantic and is served on Wedgwood's Peter Rabbit china. 'Bob's Heart Starter' is also available: a bloody Mary mix without the vodka.

Gravel paths lead to walled gardens with tennis courts, basketball and volleyball, croquet and minigolf. Once the park (strangely now pronounced Stappleford) had lions, miniature

Hambleton Hall's garden leads down to Rutland Water.

trains and liners; now it has sporting rights over 4,500 acres of hunting country and Payton aims to operate it as a stylish Victorian hunting lodge, with country house weekends available, 365 days of the year. Already on offer are shooting, fishing, riding, hunting with the Quorn and Cottesmore, and 500 acres of grounds, with their lakes and woodlands.

The setting of Hambleton Hall on a peninsula sticking out into the centre of Rutland Water gives you the impression of being cut off from the outside world. Backed by trees, the house looks down over its gardens to the water, of which there are views from the dining room and drawing room windows.

The fifteen bedrooms have been decorated by Nina Campbell and are strewn romantically around a web of corridors and stairs. Noël Coward stayed here as a friend of a previous owner, and a red and white room bears his name. 'Qazvim' has Oriental decor (unusual for a country house hotel) and an Indian-style four-poster. 'Tree top' overlooks a cedar at the front of the house; a large room utilising the ceiling slope as the line of bed draping.

In the hall are tartan-covered chairs and window-seats by a log fire. The bar has big sofas with Oriental touches and a recessed fireplace with seats in it. In the sitting room newspapers are put out on wooden poles, as in Viennese coffee-houses. The restaurant has scarlet drapes and chairs and tables clothed in white linen to the floor. The daily menu from Brian Baxter, the chef, is a single sheet with

Hambleton Hall
Hambleton, Oakham,
Rutland LE15 8TH
☎ (0572) 56991
Owners: Tim and Stefa Hart.
Member of Relais et
Châteaux
Price grid B

Location: From centre of Oakham take the A606 towards Stamford; turn right at sign to Egleton and Hambleton village only; follow the road alongside Rutland Water through the village; Hambleton Hall is signed to the right. London 90 miles. By rail from London to Kettering station which is 20 miles away.

A sundial indicates the hours of drinking at Hambleton Hall.

elegant line drawings decorating the different sections. A meal might begin with Norfolk crab on a mousse of its own dark meat with a sweet pepper sauce; continue with crispy fried scallops in their shell, or pot-roasted Norfolk squab with whole garlic cloves; and finish with Hambleton toasted rice pudding on fresh figs laced with *eau de vie*.

Recreations include trout fishing, sailing, riding, tennis, golf, shooting and hunting. Hambleton Hall issues an annual booklet on 'Things to do around Hambleton Hall', which includes local antique dealers as well as places of historical interest. The Hall itself was built in 1881 as a hunting box by a brewing magnate, Walter Marshall, who came partly for the hunting and partly for the social round in the houses of the Melton Mowbray area. Marshall was a convivial if gossipy bachelor host who left the house to his younger sister, Eva Astley Easton Cooper. After the age of fifty she became hostess to a salon of bright young things including Noël Coward and Malcolm Sargent. Of his hostess, Noël Coward wrote: 'Her principal pleasure was to lie flat on her back upon a mattress in front of the fire and shoot off witticisms in a sort of petulant wail.'

The attractive curved staircase at Congham Hall.

On arrival, guests will often find their hostess on her knees in her splendid herb garden or working on the seventeenth-century styled potager where she grows unusual vegetables for the kitchens. Visitors to this 1780 Georgian house will smell the homemade pot-pourri piled in laundry baskets by the stairs and along corridors, see dried flower arrangements from the garden, and taste some of the 130 varieties of herbs in their meals. Departing guests often say their farewells to their hostess in the greenhouse and drive away with car boots full of plants generously donated as souvenirs of their stay.

The forty acres surrounding the house include a private cricket pitch where visiting village teams play in summer, watched by house guests from the lawns near the house. There are apple orchards and meadows, and stables surrounding the house. Tennis and an outdoor pool are available.

Chef Robert Harrison goes out to the garden each evening to get inspiration for the table. He worked at the Gavroche, the Connaught and Bath's Hole in the Wall and Priory restaurants before coming to Congham a year ago. He gets his fresh fish directly from the boats in King's Lynn and not surprisingly fish and herb cookery are his favourite areas. He uses scallops and basil with a julienne of peppers, cooked in Gewürztraminer wine sauce, and King's Lynn

Congham Hall
King's Lynn, Norfolk PE32 1AH
☎ (0485) 600250
Owners: Trevor and Christine Forecast. Member of Pride of Britain
Price grid B
Notes No children under 12 years. No dogs in the hotel, but covered kennelling provided at £1 a night; stabling and hay for horses can also be provided.

Location: From King's Lynn take the A1078/A148 towards Fakenham; just after crossing the A149 turn right; the road leads down to Congham Hall.
King's Lynn 6 miles.

Part of the much-loved and well-tended gardens at Congham Hall.

shrimps, small and brown. Two local smoke houses provide more exotic tastes; and pheasant, local venison, wild duck and pigeon are usually available. Sorbets to follow a meal could be lavender flavoured. For dinner, in addition to a five-course *à la carte* meal, there is an eight course set gourmet dinner called Hobson's Choice which could centre round a main course of roast teal on a crouton with brandy-scented jus, and finish with hot plum pastry with ice-cream and a sabayon sauce.

The eleven bedrooms include a four-poster suite furnished in classical style with plenty of comforts and showers are computerized and provide instant hot water, and there is a whirl-pool bath for hire by guests for a small extra charge. Two folders of information on local sightseeing are supplied, and there is a small library of books in each room.

The Forecasts at Congham recommended me to visit Lesley Piper at Holly Lodge. The brick house dates from the six-teenth century and is a listed building. Original-ly known as Holy lodge, it was once used as a dormitory for visiting monks and friars.

The coastal area around the red-brick village of Heacham contains big beaches within six minutes' drive, backed by usually fairly de-serted pine forests and marshland. Inland villages include Burnham Thorpe, where Nel-son was born, and Peddars Way, a scenic walk which was once a Roman road.

Lesley Piper has recently hit on the most delightful way of seeing this countryside. She took a course in carriage driving at the nearby

Holly Lodge
Heacham, King's Lynn,
Norfolk PE31 7HY
☎ (0485) 70790
Owner: Mrs Lesley Piper
Price grid C
Note: Closed January and February

Location: From King's Lynn A149 coastal road towards Hunstanton; Heacham is signed on the left (turn at Norfolk Lavender corner); Holly Lodge is on the right after about 400 yards.

Holly Lodge was once a Holy Lodge, a dormitory for monks and friars.

Sandringham carriage driving centre set up by Prince Philip. She bought a carriage and two pure white Eriskay ponies, bred to pull sea-weed carts along Scottish beaches, and now hotel guests can go on outings to Sandringham or Houghton Hall, with picnic hampers for lunch.

Holly Lodge was revived by Lesley Piper about seven years ago from a delapidated private house with dry rot and no roof. She has restored six guest bedrooms with their own bathrooms. The rooms are large and quiet; the house being set in carrstone walled gardens with a large lawn. In one of the rooms the old beams and brickwork around the fireplace have been left exposed, and old bricks form a bedside table; in another a dressing table area has been created in an old fireplace.

Downstairs Lesley and her two red setters welcome guests in two sitting rooms with log fires. The pink themed dining room, consisting of two rooms linked by an archway, has walls hung with china, and dinner is served by candle-light.

A typical menu would be hot prawns in garlic cream, goujons of plaice, French onion soup or cheese soufflé; salmon steak with mustard Hollandaise, Norfolk duck with orange sauce, or fillet steak with Stilton; and there is a reasonably priced wine list.

The Old Rectory deserves inclusion, if only for its enchanting address. The spot is as sleepy as its name suggests, situated well off the busy main road and approached down lanes where high hedges

The fifteenth century rectory at Great Snoring has finely decorated brick work on its walls.

conceal the fields. Secluded in its 1½ acres of sheltered garden, the Old Rectory is an impressive house. Creeper crawls over elaborate decorative brickwork; round the south-east window a terracotta frieze shows male and female heads; and heraldic symbols are found on the oak front door. It has old mullioned windows with leaded glass, and little turrets and tall chimneys. It dates from 1500, when it was built as the hexagonal home of Sir Ralph Shilton.

The house has a well polished look, with gleaming silver and china, and antique chests and tables. Drinks can be taken in the sitting room; and in the dining room, with its mullioned windows and heavy oak beams, traditional English dishes are served and there is a reasonably priced wine list of about twenty or so wines. Popular dishes are cream of celery soup with Stilton, smoked goose breast with black cherry, mackerel pâté with ginger roast, fillet of beef Wellington, roast leg of pork with apricot sauce, steak, kidney and mushroom pie, casserole of venison, Queen of Puddings, apple and walnut crumble and hot lemon pudding.

Trees shelter Otley House but to one side in the three acres of grounds there is a small lake with ducks and moorhens, a putting green and an especially well-kept croquet lawn.

The big hall has an information table, an open fire, a grandfather clock and blue and white china on the overmantel. The Queen Anne staircase leads up to the Victorian period back section and five double rooms. Downstairs there is an elegant drawing room, another separate one for smokers, and a billiards room

The Old Rectory
Barsham Road, Great Snoring, Fakenham, Norfolk NR21 0HF
☎ (032872) 820597
Owners: William and Rosamund Scoles
Price grid C
Notes No children under 12 years. No pets.

Location: Take the A148 from King's Lynn towards Fakenham; left towards Great Snoring. In village, continue along main street past the church and turn left into Barsham Road; the Old Rectory is on the left behind a high wall.

A bedroom at Otley Park.

with a ten-foot table, leather chairs and sofa and an open fire. The dining room facing the lawn has Regency furniture around the communal polished table, a chandelier and a grand piano which guests are welcome to play. Danish-born Lise Hilton is an excellent cook serving many Scandinavian as well as English dishes. Lise opened the house after her sons had grown up and has learnt as she has gone along, but her house has now been voted the best bed and breakfast in East Anglia. Dinner is a set menu with Lise and Mike joining guests when they can. Lise will also prepare something different for those who cannot eat what is on the menu.

The exterior of this Grade II listed house is Georgian, and the inside is mainly furnished in Regency style, but was mentioned as a manor back in 1528. Like most Danes, Lise loves candles and the rooms are filled with candlelight in the evenings reflecting along with the flames of the open fires off collections of pig figures, china and pewter.

T he approach to Hintlesham Hall, past a screen of huge trees and a white chain fence protecting the lawn, shows off its façade to perfection. In the evening the buttermilk and white frontage catches the sun. The façade is Georgian, added in 1720, but the steep roof, dormer windows and chimneys show an earlier Dutch influence.

Ruth and David Watson bought Hintlesham in 1984 from Robert Carrier and are putting all their efforts into making it as perfect as possible. Ruth Watson keeps a housewifely eye on everything, from the health of the plants in huge pots lining the entrance hall's black and white tiled floor to ensuring the local bookshop supplies her with the latest books to put in guests' rooms. She has put together a booklet, for the benefit of guests, containing her personal choice of Suffolk antique shops, eating places, villages and local sights.

Ruth also sends out a seasonal newsletter detailing what is going on at the Hall, such as cookery demonstrations, the Guy Fawkes Night celebration with its huge firework display, dinner and dancing evenings, and the Newmarket racing calendar. She also organizes all-day croquet tournaments, having delivered copies of the basic rules to guests' rooms in advance. There is tuition on two croquet lawns, and on the day there is a picnic lunch, or buffet if wet, Pimms on tap for the afternoon's play, a tea of cucumber sandwiches and scones and a four-course dinner for those players still speaking to each other.

Such events make Hintlesham a friendlier and more enjoyable place than the formal

Otley House
Otley, Ipswich, Suffolk
IP6 9NR
☎ (0473) 39253
Owners: Mike and Lise Hilton. Members of Wolsey Lodge.
Price grid C
Notes: Closed mid-November to beginning of March. No children under 12 years; no pets; no smoking in the bedrooms.

Location: From Ipswich take the B1077 Westerfield Road; go over level crossing, through Westerfield village, and continue through Winesham; leaving Winesham, look out for phone box on right and take next right towards Swilland; continue through Swilland to Otley T-junction; Otley House is straight ahead.

Hintlesham Hall
near Ipswich, Suffolk
IP6 JNS
☎ (047 387) 334/268
Owners: David and Ruth Watson
General Manager: Tim Sutherland. Member of Relais et Châteaux
Price grid B
Note: Kennelling in the grounds.

Location: From London area take the M11, the M25 east, and the A12 to Chelmsford and past Colchester; approaching Ipswich look out for roundabout with huge Tesco store; go straight on for a few hundred yards; at traffic lights, with Post House on left, turn left on to A1071 to Hadleigh; at small roundabout go straight on ⅔ mile, through Hintlesham village; the Hall is signed to the right on a sharp left-hand bend.

*The Georgian facade of
Hintlesham Hall looks
glorious in the sun.*

furniture and architecture might suggest. Around the open fires are pleasant areas where you can put together one of the jig-saw puzzles provided, play Scrabble or just subside into a sofa. There are seventeen bedrooms at present, and plans for a possible coach-house and stable conversion to create more. The hand-carved oak staircase is attributed to Grinling Gibbons. Victorian children appear in paintings hung on Sanderson Tiffany wallpaper by the stairs. The larger rooms on the first floor include the Rosette room, with its four-poster, French toile canopy and drapings, seventeenth-century carved stone fireplace and overmantel, and an oval eighteenth-century-style painting of the house commissioned by Robert Carrier. The writing desk is eighteenth-century, as are the tripod tables. The Carolean room opposite can either serve as a guest lounge or form part of a suite with Austrian white pine panelling and carved eighteenth-century mantel. The ceiling is a rare example of sixteenth-century undercut plaster work. Each room has a small refrigerator, bar, radio, colour television, hair-drier, robes, biscuits, direct-dial telephone and plenty of toiletries to bring one to today. The upper rooms are equally attractive if not so stately in size. 'Ravillious', for example, has beamed sloping walls, pale beige fabrics, books, glossy magazines, Victorian prints on the walls and views of the garden and trout lake. In the garden there is also a tennis court, a large grey gelding to ride, clay pigeon shooting, and boats on the stream running by. In the library there is a full-sized billiards table.

Chef Alan Ford, who worked with Mosimann at the Dorchester, provides suitably elegant food for the dining room, with its reproduction Louis XVI chairs and Edwardian portraits.

Owner Gerald Milsom, who founded the Pride of Britain organisation and the Taste of England scheme, has worked long and hard to create an image of good hotels and food in rural England. From the entrance of the Victorian Maison Talbooth he will point with pride to the view down over the Dedham valley, unaltered since Constable painted it. One can still go to see Willy Lott's cottage, which appears in 'The Haywain' and 'Flatford Mill'. The Milsom family restaurant, Le Talbooth, in a sixteenth-century timbered building which was once a weaver's cottage, is right on the River Stour (half a mile away), and can be seen in the Constable painting 'Dedham Vale'. This is where guests at the Maison go to dine. An alternative place to eat is at the conservatory-style Terrace restaurant in the Dedham Vale Hotel, which is in the same village and under the same ownership. If you are out touring, the Pier restaurant at Harwich is another Milsom place, where you can enjoy seafood and watch the North Sea ferries.

The Maison is a spacious Victorian house with bedrooms named after English poets and especially large and sumptuous bathrooms. The huge Shakespeare suite with its blue canopied bed has a circular bath and a patio. 'Keats' also has a patio, a canopied half-tester bed and white conservatory-style chairs and tables for room service (breakfast and snacks only are provided). 'Shelley' has lovely views and a large corner Jacuzzi in the bathroom.

The Maison has no reception area though it was one of the pioneer country house hotels, converted in 1969. The name, like that of the restaurant, dates from around 1786, when tolls were collected at the bridge from road and river users.

Maison Talbooth
Stratford Road, Colchester, Essex CO7 6HN
☎ (0206) 322367
Owner: Gerald Milsom.
Member of Pride of Britain
Price grid B

Location: From Colchester take the A12 towards Ipswich; turn off at sign to Stratford St Mary past the Talbooth restaurant right over the dual carriageway at top of hill (you have to go right through the village at present as road subsidence has blocked way in near hotel).

Le Talbooth Restaurant where guests eat at Maison Talbooth was featured in a Constable painting.

WALES
AND THE BORDERS

The Empty Quarters

The Elms at Abberley was designed by a pupil of Sir Christopher Wren.

It is perverse how the English (and others), in their attempts to escape the crowds for open rugged hills and wild and windy walks, almost invariably go plunging way up north to the Highlands and islands of northern Scotland, covering several hundreds of weary miles in their lemming flight.

A more approachable bolt-hole, thanks to the motorway links, is mid-Wales, where the county of Powys has a very low population count. It is a place of hills, deep valleys, purposefully moving streams and drovers' roads, where you can walk watched only by sheep and rare red kites. On the other side of Wales is Pembrokeshire, where wild flowers bloom earlier than in eastern England, abounding in unsprayed hedgerows; there is also the Pembroke national park, with a coastal path to walk. To the north are the soaring shapes of Snowdonia, its little steam railways, castles and gardens.

Cardiff, the Welsh capital, is a prosperous boom city at the moment, but small enough to get around easily on foot. Here you can shop without crowds and protected from the weather in Victorian arcades containing branches of national chains. The heart of the city is Cardiff Castle, the richly gilded, carved and coloured medieval fantasy dwelling created by the Victorian architect William Burges for the Marques of Bute, whose family built Cardiff docks and made the coast the world's foremost exporter of coal. Castel Coch, the red castle, six miles away near the M4, is another fairy tale invention: the nineteenth-century recreation of a thirteenth-century French castle, complete with dungeons where the only recorded prisoner was Alan Ladd; the castle naturally makes a perfect movie set.

If one turns right and north after entering the Principality from the Severn bridge, one can explore the Wye valley, which offers salmon, white water rapids around Symonds Yat and the ruins of Tintern Abbey, and feel the exhilaration of walking or pony trekking in the Brecon Beacons.

The Eppint hills leading down to Brecon are high and empty. The road here was once the last stretch of the drover's route as they moved their sheep down to the Brecon market. The now closed Drovers Arms, resting-place for sheep and drovers, is still marked – one of few signs of human occupation – on the map of the hills.

Just as Wales has been little penetrated by the mass visitor, so too the Marches or Borders have been neglected and still form unspoilt traditional rural areas of England; Herefordshire and Shropshire are counties of

Previous pages: Llanrhaeadr Hall blends Tudor and Georgian wings with a Georgian facade.

calm little villages, with black and white timbered houses, and scenery beloved of A.E.
Housman. Crafts survive here: cheese, wine
and cider making, herb and flower drying,
weaving, wood carving, hedge laying, wild life
management. On a short visit it may be difficult
to get to the heart-of-the-country lore quickly,
so Janet and Nicholas Kyrle-Pope arrange day
visits or short breaks in Herefordshire meeting
craftsmen and local people with accommodation to suit individual tastes. They are based
at Much Marcle, Ledbury, Herefordshire
HR8 2NU (053184 606), which is handy for
those staying at Hope End.

The traveller cannot plead lack of accommodation as an excuse for failing to explore
these empty quarters. Wales has a good
selection of country house hotels, and more are
on the way. Llangoed Castle is owned and being
decorated by Laura Ashley's family, who have
close ties with Wales. There are enough
country house hotels to enable a travel expert
like Emyr Griffiths to produce his Welsh
Rarebits programme, which offers an individual
booking service for carefully selected hotels all
over Wales.

The Elms is a Queen Anne residence set
in twelve acres in rolling hill country
with views of the Malvern Hills. It dates
from 1710 and was originally designed by a pupil
of Sir Christopher Wren, Gilbert White. The
house is named after the elms that once lined
the carriageway, long since replaced by limes.
The grounds include a large kitchen garden, and
a herb garden, as well as croquet, tennis and

*A stained glass window at
The Elms.*

putting. The Elms became a hotel in 1946 and now has 25 rooms (9 of them in a converted stable block) furnished with comfortable antiques. Three sitting rooms with log fires are where coffee and afternoon tea are served. The library bar still has its carved wooden mantelpiece and old mahogany bookcases; here light lunches are served by an open fire. Over the fireplace are the coat of arms of former owner Sir Richard Brooke, after whom the restaurant is named. The candle-lit dining room is in Regency style, and has an open fireplace. Sometimes there is a classical guitarist to provide entertainment while diners enjoy such dishes as lambs' tongues braised with port in a pastry case, rich rabbit pâté with home-made chutney and toasted brioche, and fillet steak fried and served with grated parsnip on a red wine and vinegar butter sauce. Puddings may be steamed treacle pudding with custard, lemon tart, or raspberry mousse on a shortbread base with cream sauce. Chef John Daniels previously worked at Billesley Manor, and his work is influenced by the availability of produce from the herb garden, and the fruit farms in the nearby Vale of Evesham.

The Elms
Stockton Road, Abberley, near Worcester WR6 6AT
☎ (0299) 896666
Proprietors: Norfolk Capital
General Manager: Cecilia Rydstrom
Hotels. Member of Prestige
Price grid B

Location: 15 minutes from Exit 5, 6 or 7 of M5. Taking Exit 7, go to Worcester; then take the A443 towards Tenbury Wells; The Elms is on the right of this road just after the B4202 turning on right.
Helicopter pad.

Hope End is the wrong name for this enchanting and eccentric house, secreted in a sheltered dip among trees and walled gardens. The house is a happy place, and has given new life and hopes to its present owners, who gave up their jobs to labour on its restoration from a decaying apple store.

The house is basically eighteenth-century, with minarets inspired by the Royal Pavilion at Brighton, looking somewhat bizarre in this lush English country setting. These Oriental touches were added by Edward Moulton Barrett, Elizabeth Barrett Browning's father, whose family lived here for twenty years. Papa had made his fortune in the Jamaica sugar plantations and hired John Loudon, a Regency landscape architect, to lay out the 470-acre estate and park using a series of hidden valleys. When Edward Moulton Barrett built a more lavish Oriental house nearby, the original house was made into stables. Now it has been restored back to house and hotel by former solicitor John Hegarty and his wife Patricia. Elizabeth Barrett Browning reflected the impression Hope End made on her in her poem 'The Lost Bower':

> Green the land is where my daily
> Steps in jocund childhood played
> Dimpled close with hill and valley
> Dappled very close with shade
> Summer-snow of apple-blossoms running up
>   from glade to glade.

Hope End Country House Hotel
Hope End, Ledbury, Herefordshire HR5 1JQ
☎ (0531) 3613
Owners: John and Patricia Hegarty
Price grid A (includes five-course dinner)
Notes: Closed Monday and Tuesday nights each week; and from last weekend in November to last weekend in February.

Location: From M50 take Exit 2 A417 to Ledbury; then right to Hope End, or from Worcester A449 to Ledbury.

Hope End has changed little, land-locked in its forty acres of grounds. Apart from the working garden, guests can walk in parkland, which is listed as historic, and through bluebell woods. The Hegarty's have replanted the vegetable, fruit and herb gardens; they even have their own spring water to complete their 'good life'. Patricia's whole-food cooking earns her many accolades. The room price includes her five-course dinner and breakfast of home-baked breads, eggs from her own hens, yoghurts from her own goats' milk and home-made preserves. Patricia now produces sixty different vegetables, fifty different herbs and forty varieties of apple, as well as other fruits from her acre of walled garden. Game and meat come from local farmers. Her dinner menus start with unusual soup blends: carrot and coriander, spinach and coconut, beetroot and artichoke; or *hors d'oeuvres* like Queen scallops in saffron and yoghurt sauce, hake and lobster hot pots, lambs' kidneys in sherry and thyme sauce. The main course could be roast duckling with gooseberry sauce, roast fillet of pork with cider sauce, or whiting in perry and cardoon sauce. A salad follows the main course, then a choice of three farm cheeses. While the choice of puddings might include Great Granny's wine and lemon velvet cream, rose-petal apple sorbet, lime tart, pears baked in perry with vine leaves, or almond tart and mulberry sauce. Vegetarian meals are available by arrangement. Patricia has recently written a book entitled *An English Flavour*, containing her own recipes.

The house has been furnished in a light and airy style, underlining the country feel. The

Hope End was the childhood home of Elizabeth Barrett Browning.

main sitting room has huge Georgian windows, big plain sofas and plenty of books. The dining room has the same floor-to-ceiling windows, modern prints, plain light wooden tables and matching armchairs. There is also another sitting room, decorated with dried flowers and bookshelves, where little Victorian velvet chairs and a miniature chest make a cosy place to sit by a brick-lined wood stove.

The Hegartys blend eighteenth-century English country oak with hand-made modern items from local craftsmen. They have hand-loomed woollen fabrics made to their own designs in a small mill in Wales. There are nine guest rooms, two of which are in the grounds, including the very private garden cottage suite rustically set next to the walled garden.

Close proximity to an international airport does not suggest tranquillity for a country house hotel. However, once you leave those thatched cottages behind, peace begins. You notice the view before the house itself. It looks down a valley, shielded by trees to one side, to the high arches of a listed railway viaduct (still used); those arches in turn frame a country park backing a beach which is popular with sailing and windsurfing enthusiasts; in the distance is a little island, now a bird sanctuary.

Egerton Grey was rechristened for its new secular life as a hotel. It used to be the rectory for the little church at Porthkerry, to which a path leads uphill. It was built in the days when parsons lived well. A Bath architect designed it, and its stone façade suggests the Cotswolds.

Egerton Grey looks down the valley to the sea behind clerical yew hedges.

Egerton Grey
Porthkerry, South
Glamorgan CF6 9BZ
☎ (0446) 711666
Owners: Bart and Iris Zuzik.
Listed in Welsh Rarebits
Price grid C

Location: Leave M4 at Exit 33; take the A4232 south, signed Cardiff airport (A4050); take the A4226 towards Porthkerry; after ⅕ mile there are four thatched cottages on the left of the road; turn into the lane between second and third cottages; Egerton Grey is on the left at the end of the lane, 10 miles from Exit 33. By rail to Cardiff.

A Japanese statue in the grounds of Egerton Grey.

The Zuziks found a reference to Grey Egerton in the title deeds, and switched the name around; it now sounds like the hero of a Regency novel. The house is set back behind clerical yew hedges above terraced gardens with croquet lawn, tennis court and a kitchen garden at the side. It dates from three main periods: seventeenth, nineteenth and twentieth centuries, all well blended. One rings at the door for entrance, to be greeted by Amy, the Zuzik's daughter, who manages the hotel. Amy escorts arrivals to their rooms, indicated by nicknames referring to their position, view or family associations, for example 'Uncle Fred's room'; but the guest will find his or her own name on a white card on the door. The Zuziks hired a professional designer to marry rich tapestry and chintz fabrics to the period rooms; and books, magazines, china, paintings and framed family photographs are highlighted by freshly arranged flowers. Amy's toys are piled in an old cradle at the top of the stairs, and can be borrowed to cuddle at night. Bowls of fruit are also placed on the landing for guests.

Not that anyone is likely to be lonely or hungry in this mellow, happy household. The Zuziks have long had a reputation in Cardiff for their American, bottomless coffee-pot kind of hospitality, dating from the days when they ran the only Cardiff bed and breakfast hotel to rate a *Michelin* mention. Iris was born in Cardiff, and Bart was a hospital administrator in Chicago. They bought Egerton Grey because they needed a new challenge, and spent the winter camped in the 1920 library with only a fire for company while new plumbing and electrics were put in and restoration carried out, which included the old servants' quarters being turned into what is now a honeymooners' delight: a secluded room under the roof, with beamed and sloping ceiling. The old nursery has a balcony with a view of the sea; and one master bedroom has its own small dressing room leading to a delightful long room centred round a massive deep blue claw-footed tub with a wrap-round shower stall at one end. On cold days gas 'log' fires are lit in the guest rooms, heavy curtains drawn, and the arriving traveller is greeted with a reviving tray of tea and Welsh griddle scones.

Egerton Grey favours Welsh produce where possible. There is Welsh mineral water at the side of the bed, that can be a 1784 four-poster or a William and Mary half-tester. Local meat and fish are bought; wine is served in Welsh crystal, and food on Royal Worcester. Local ladies are helping to re-establish the herb garden; and the cheese board is all Welsh, even if the Stilton costs more than the English version.

At dinner, tables are personalized with guests' names on handwritten menus. Chef Paul Whittock, previously with Charingworth Manor and Ettington Park serves an à la carte menu based on the finest English and French traditions. Rack of Welsh lamb with spinach comes on a garlic cream sauce; the choice of desserts may include hot strawberries with caramelized orange and green peppercorns, or lemon flan with hazelnut praline. On Sunday a traditional lunch is served, and non-resident guests tend to stay on for tea and often even into the evening, playing card and board games, reading or playing croquet.

When someone makes a booking Michael Yates is careful to send directions. It is not that the hotel is difficult to find; in this unpeopled part of mid-Wales the choice of houses is few. But it is also rare to find many people around to ask the way, and if you do, can you pronounce this Welsh tongue-bedeviller? Yates suggest saying 'Loo-in-derr-oo' with the accent on the *derr*. For the nearby town of Llanwrtyd Wells, a former spa which prides itself on being the smallest town in Britain, with a population of six hundred, he suggests uttering 'la naughty dwells' very quickly.

Llwynderw means 'oak wood', and this 1796 farmhouse, though a thousand feet up and with moorland all around, certainly has a snug setting: it has its back close up against a steep hill and looks down a quiet valley in the heart of what once was drovers' country and still is good sheep land. Yates accepts no tours, parties or conferences and says that here his guests rediscover silence. Azaleas, rhododendrons and lilies bloom, and eighty species of bird have been spotted in the gardens. The rooms have country furniture and antiques and fresh bright fabrics; the eye is drawn down to the valley views in the front.

Michael Yates lists his house rules behind the bathroom door. You ring the bell at reception on arrival for service. There is no bar, but drinks are served at any time, along with tea or coffee. The front door is shut at 11 p.m.: 'country hours are kept at Llwynderw'. For late-night chats there is the Palm Court with its own spring and fountain. The water is acid, so soda has been added to stop corrosion of the pipes. The local water is so pure that frogs love it, and their spawn is sought by English counties where frogs are scarce.

The host's bark is worse than his bite. The house is relaxed, and after a day's walking or touring – or even just getting there – few want to carouse all night. Drinks before and after

Llwynderw
Abergwesyn, Llanwrtyd Wells, Powys LD5 4TW
☎ (059 13) 238
Owner: Michael Yates. Member of Pride of Britain
Price grid C
Note: Closed sometimes in winter; check first

Location: From Brecon take B4520 and B4519 to A483; left to Llanwrtyd Wells. At Neuadd Arms hotel take left turn to Abergwesyn and the hotel will be found signed on left hand side of the road.

Llwynderw is set snugly against the hills.

dinner are taken by the fire in a book-filled sitting room, one of two, or out on the terrace when the weather is fine. The menu is displayed at reception each day, and guests should order wines in advance. The dining room looks to the side of the garden and is dominated by a huge fireplace, with oak beam over it, installed by Yates. Here an inscription in classical Welsh declares that the house was built in 1796 and 'addwrnwyd' (adorned) by Yates in 1969.

His dining room adornments include a painting of geraniums by Thea Dupays of Hunstrete House and a high pointed Welsh hat over the door. Candle-light yellows off the wooden tables. A Spanish chef creates excellent set meals, including wonderful soups with second helpings offered; I had a marvellous smitane sauce with roast quail on a crouton, garnished with fried breadcrumbs and accompanied by side platter of vegetables. A green salad comes before a choice of puddings: hot treacle tart, apricot soufflé, creme caramel. Two cheeses, deliberately small in choice to ensure freshness, are offered: usually Stilton and Cheddar. Breakfast is served on gingham and Masons stoneware country china. The uncooked dishes are set out in buffet fashion, with a huge plaited loaf to cut as you wish, and home-made marmalades and preserves.

Caer Beris, 'the fortress on the rock', was the home of Lord Swansea at the end of the nineteenth century and is said to be haunted by his widow. The house has an elaborate mock-Tudor façade with black and white timbering, chimney breasts cutting through the sides of the house, steep roofs and gables and a big courtyard. The other side of the house reflects its name and is supported on pillars over terraced gardens which drop sheer to the River Irfon opposite a large caravan site.

Caer Beris on its river curve has 27 acres of fishing rights and runs fishing packages on the River Wye. Caer Beris lake is a hundred yards from the hotel and well stocked with rainbow and brook trout. The fishing on the hotel's own river stretch is free and reserved exclusively for guests. It is good fishing; salmon, brown

Caer Beris
Builth Wells, Powys
☎ (0982) 552601
Owner: Pete Smith
Price grid C

Location: Take the A40 west from Abergavenny, then the A429 and A470 to Builth Wells; through town and out on the A483 towards Garth; take first turning on the left (signed) to the hotel after crossing the river bridge.

and rainbow trout, dace, chub and pike are all caught here. Walking holidays run by the Welsh Wanderers company are based on this hotel, with walks to the upper Wye valley to see herons, buzzards and salmon.

The house which was becoming somewhat rundown and slightly frayed at the edges, has recently been restored by photographer Pete Smith who has got rid of the chain hotel furniture in the 22 bedrooms and replaced it with countrified antiques in keeping with the style of the house.

The drawing room is pillared and very Edwardian in design. The dining room has sixteenth-century oak panelling, and has arms of Lord Swansea over the large stone fireplace. Chef Graham Ruchat serves Welsh lamb with a Brecon whisky sauce, fillet of beef Prince of Wales – four thin fillets, two with mild curry sauce, and two with a creamy white wine sauce; navarin of Welsh lamb comes in stout sauce, and there is always a vegetarian dish among the main course choices.

Caer Beris means 'the fortress on the rock' and stands high above the River Irfon.

W hereas Caer Beris may have been a splendid copy of Welsh black and white timbering, Trelydan Hall is the real thing. It stands proudly Tudor on the foundations of a medieval hospice, itself built on the site of a Roman villa called Latao (meaning 'lying hidden').

Until late 1988 it was owned by Mrs Ioan Trevor-Jones, who for forty years was a professional lecturer and flower arranger on cruise ships such as the QE2. She created the superb gardens that lead down to the house, including a water garden, and with tender plants growing in the shelter of a twelve-foot wall dating from 1770. In early May there are tree peonies from China in bloom, and golden South American lilies by the lakeside, and there is a superb collection of Eastern Mediterranean hellebores. Snowdrops, wild daffodils and bluebells abound in Spring, and purple crocuses give colour in autumn. A hundred years ago the garden was famous, and Mrs Trevor-Jones spent a decade re-establishing it.

The pure Elizabethan ambience continues inside the house, though the rooms have modern bathrooms. The Welsh oak suite has a wooden floor, carpeted with rugs, and a ceiling-high four-poster; the drawing room suite has a sitting area next to a fireplace. Suites in the Georgian and Victorian wings can be rented for self-catering.

Trelydan Hall
Welshpool, Powys
☎ (0938) 2773
Owner: (the hall has been placed on the market at time of going to press but it is understood that it will be kept and developed as a hotel and the gardens maintained)
Previous price grid C

Location: From Welshpool take A490 towards Llanfyllin: on the right just outside Welshpool take Windmill lane up hill and follow signs to the hall along narrowing tracks through farmland.

O ne of the most popular attractions of North Wales are its miniature railways with their toy-like little steam trains,

Tudor Trelydan Hall shows off the Welsh art of black and white timbering.

A carving detail from the sideboard in the board room at Pale Hall.

originally built as work-horses for quarrying and mining. The most famous line is the Blaenau Festiniog, which runs from Blaenau down to the coast at Porthmadog and used to carry slate, each piece chipped out by hand in the quarries. There are two working quarries which run tours for visitors; meals are served on board the train, and carriages can be hired for private parties.

A hotel closely associated with railways and their history is Pale Hall, built in an ostentatious Victorian baronial style by a railway baron. A derelict railway track runs along the lower edge of the hotel's parkland along the banks of the Dee (that flows on to Chester). The track, now without its rails, makes a peaceful walk, with primroses lining its banks in spring.

Pale Hall was built in 1870 by Scotsman Henry Robertson, an engineer. He pulled down the original house, after trying to restore it, and gave his architects unlimited funds. Pale was his home until his death in 1888.

Robertson had worked with Robert Stevenson, and the Brymbo coalfields asked him to come to North Wales to make a report on a possible railway. Robertson became involved and was the engineer on the construction in the late 1840s of the Shrewsbury to Chester line, which involved building viaducts over the Dee and Ceiriog rivers. The railway was opposed by landowners, and often he had to survey proposed routes secretly at night. His work in Wales encouraged him to build Pale as his home, which he left to his only son, Henry, who was knighted by Queen Victoria in 1890.

Pale Hall
Llandderfel, Bala, Gwynedd
☎ (067 83) 285
Owner: Mr and Mrs Tim Ovens
Price grid C

Location: Take the A5 from Shrewsbury; turn left at its branch with A494 going towards Bala; turn left on B4402 to Llandderfel; go through village and left to Pale.

Queen Victoria visited Pale in 1889, and liked the area; the path she took along the Dee is still called the Queen's Walk. Staying at Pale one can use the bath the good queen cleaned in and the adjoining bedroom is complete with antique half-tester bed. Sir Henry Robertson created a rock garden of rare plants in Pale's 16-acre grounds, and ran a trout hatchery. Now solid swathes of daffodils surround the house in spring. After becoming a military hospital and then a school, the house lay empty for twenty years before it became a hotel in 1983.

As one enters the house from the side, the high wooden-vaulted Victorian hall looks most lordly. Paintings hang above it and a big open fire is the setting for afternoon tea with rich home-made cakes. Opening off the hall is the Boudoir, with a hand-painted domed ceiling and now a no smoking area, and a bar ingeniously fashioned from marble fireplaces taken out when bathrooms were put in. The gold and green dining room with its gold ceiling, Italian carved chairs, huge gilded mirror and silver door furniture is the sumptuous setting for dishes like cheese soufflé on leek sauce, hot sticky toffee pudding and Pale ice cream.

The 15 bedrooms and 2 suites with their local place-names are very individually furnished; 'Caernarvon' has a round bed and Jacuzzi, 'Beaumaris' a four-poster and spa bath. The bathrooms have equally flamboyant decor, with stepped-up baths and bowls of heart-shaped soaps. The hotel also has a spa bath, a plunge pool, sauna solarium, and exercise equipment. Thirty miles of fishing rights on the Dee are available to guests.

Pale Hall where Queen Victoria stayed in 1890.

Historic House Hotels is a private company dedicated to the rescue and restoration of architecturally important country houses in order to convert them into hotels of great comfort and standard. They don't aim to be a big chain. Bodysgallen, opened in 1982, was their first hotel, Middlethorpe (see page 165), the second and Hartwell House (see page 29) their latest venture.

Bodysgallen (pronounced Bodysgathlen) centres round a thirteenth-century tower looking down on Conwy and its castle and the big Victorian resort of Llandudno. Bodnant gardens are nearby, and Betws-y-Coed and the 840 square miles of the Snowdonia National Park can be seen in the distance from the windows.

The park and secluded hill lakes for fishing, like Llyn Crafant above Trefriw, are good places for days out with a picnic hamper. Bodysgallen provides plenty of tranquillity of its own. The name has been interpreted as the 'house among the thistles' or 'the house of Caswallon' (who died in 517). The house, built mainly in the seventeenth century, is set in parkland on a hillside. The tower is reached by a narrow winding stone staircase once used as a look-out by soldiers serving the English kings of Conwy. The bedrooms curl around this core, approached by many little landings and corridors. Rooms contain restful, comfortable furniture. There are window-seats or deep chairs where you can sit with book and biscuits and look out over the gardens to the mountains. Each room has a desk, with plants, flowers and plenty of writing paper.

In the oak-panelled entrance hall and lounge there is always a fire burning, with a cunning draught gadget to blow hot air back into the room. There are magazines, papers and information sheets to read over a Welsh tea of scones, home-made jam and date and walnut cakes. On the first floor is a second oak-panelled drawing room with a magnificent fireplace and mullioned windows, and hung with seventeenth- and eighteenth-century portraits.

The house has its outdoor drawing rooms too. It has seven acres of gardens and 43 acres of park and woodland. Near the house there is an eighteenth-century walled rose garden and a rare Dutch seventeenth-century knot garden in geometric patterns of clipped box hedge with sweet-scented herbs. Cottages and outbuildings have been converted to self-contained accommodation, some containing sitting rooms and kitchenettes.

Head chef Martin James includes traditional Celtic, Welsh and Scottish culinary ideas in his menus. Bodysgallen terrine is pheasant and chicken livers in port jelly; a saddle of Welsh

Bodysgallen Hall
Llandudno, Gwynedd
LL30 1RS
☎ (0492) 84466
Owners: Historic House Hotels. Member of Prestige; listed in Welsh Rarebits.
Price grid B
Notes: Children under 8 years at management discretion. Dogs only in cottage suites.

Location: A55/A546 from Chester towards Llandudno; just before main centre of Llandudno turn left on to the B5115, then left on to the A470 towards Llandudno Junction; Bodysgallen is on the left.
By rail to Llandudno Junction, where guests can be met.

The seventeenth-century Dutch knot garden at Bodysgallen Hall. The low, clipped, box hedges surround sweet scented herbs.

lamb comes Wellington-style; and the choice of puddings might be blackcurrant parfait with blackcurrant sauce, or hot coconut and sultana tart with chocolate sauce.

Llanrhaeadr was once famous for its healing spring water. It makes a good touring centre, handy for Ruthin and Denbigh, both places having thirteenth-century castles; within 40 minutes of Betws-y-Coed, and half an hour from Chester, where you can shop in its unique medieval 'rows'. St Asaph, boasting the smallest cathedral in England and Wales, is also nearby.

Llanrhaeadr Hall has a dignified Georgian façade and three acres of grounds. It was enlarged in the eighteenth century by Richard Parry, the high sheriff of Merioneth, Caernarvon and Denbigh, who wanted a more imposing house in keeping with his status. He went to Robert Adam for designs, and one can see four drawings in the Adam collection at the Sir John Soane Museum in London. Neither of the two plans he prepared was built, probably because of the cost; instead an elegant Georgian extension was added to the Tudor house. The ground floor has an Adam-style staircase, and a dining room with quarter panelling, mahogany doors and Adam-style fireplaces, though some of the latter have now disappeared. A later owner with a fondness for the Jacobean period put a Jacobean look on the south façade, and brought the Georgian extension more in keeping with the whole design.

Philip and Elaine Catlow say they are running a country house with hotel service. The dozen bedrooms, named after Welsh castles,

Llanrhaeadr Hall
Llanrhaeadr, near Denbigh, Clwyd, N. Wales
☎ (074 578) 313
Owners: Philip and Elaine Catlow. Listed in Welsh Rarebits.
Price grid C
Notes: Children under 8 years by arrangement. Dogs provided with kennels and food overnight for a small charge.

Location: Llanrhaeadr is half-way between Denbigh and Ruthin on the A825.

are mostly generous in size and modern in appearance. Maggie, the Irish wolfhound, greets new arrivals in the rather dark hall. The large drawing room with its Adam-style fireplace is hung with tapestries and chandeliers and has a hundred-year-old Steinway grand piano. The Georgian dining room, from which there are hill views, has a Welsh dresser and ladder-backed chairs. Philip Catlow's dishes have been given Shakespearean names: Falstaff's terrine is house pâté with smoked chicken and wild duck; soufflé Cleopatra is Lymeswold cheese in an English pancake, topped with blackcurrant sauce; smoked venison Richard III is strips of venison with a little melon; pudding à la Sir Toby Belch is a steamed sponge with custard; savouries are also served.

Soughton is approached along a stunning avenue of limes and through a courtyard entrance. From its building in 1714 until its sale to the present owners in 1986, Soughton was the home of the Wynne Banks family, whose members included a bishop, two knights, three high sheriffs, a chaplain to Queen Victoria, a Lord Chief Justice, a Lord Chancellor's secretary and William John Banks, one of the great early nineteenth-century travellers and collectors, whose book on exploring the Amazon still makes thrilling reading. He remodelled Soughton in the 1820s, adding roof pavilions, mullioned windows and Islamic turrets. The plans were drawn up by a contemporary traveller, Sir Charles Barry, who later designed the Houses of Parliament.

When the Rodenhursts bought the property it was unfurnished, the roof leaked, there was dry rot, and the plumbing and electrics were old; but within a year the house was restored with period interiors and charming decorations chosen by Mrs Rodenhurst. The library, lined with books and leather sofas, leads from the entrance hall to the Justice bar, a small room through a concealed door in a bookcase. The bar was originally the courtroom of the high sheriffs of Flintshire and has a marble corner fireplace with elaborate coat of arms over it,

Soughton Hall
Northrop, near Chester, Clwyd CH7 6AB
☎ (035286) 207/484
Owners: John and Rosemary Rodenhurst. Member of Pride of Britain. Listed in Welsh Rarebits.
Price grid B

Location: From Chester take the A55, signed to Conwy, until you reach the traffic signals at Northrop village; turn left here and follow signs to Soughton Hall.

Soughton Hall had islamic turrets added to it by its Victorian owner.

The first-floor drawing room at Soughton Hall.

depicting heaven and hell. Behind the hall, the ladies' room is the former butlers' pantry with its original cupboards and bells for servants to answer. The old servants' hall is used for breakfast service, and lunch in winter.

The Soughton parlour with its chinoiserie panels is used for private meetings. At the top of the eighteenth-century well staircase, carved in oak, are the formal first-floor reception rooms, added by Banks. The drawing room has oak panelling and a high gilt ceiling; the walls are hung with copies of the Dame au Licorne French tapestries. The dining room is noble with double windows from floor to ceiling, hung with huge drapes; and on a gleaming wood floor there are polished antique tables and Chippendale style chairs beneath a ceiling painted with an original 1820 cameo in oil. The chef, Malcolm Warham, used to work at Eastwell Manor. On each day of the week he produces a traditional roast and an old-fashioned pudding of the day, as well as home-made ice-creams and a selection of British farmhouse cheese and fruit. A gourmet dinner menu is also available.

The bedrooms all have the original names that appear beside the bells in the old pantry. They have been charmingly and even wittily furnished by Mrs Rodenhurst, with floral patterned toilet bowls and basins in the Edwardian-style bathrooms. The master bedroom has a four-poster with lace drapes falling from a crown. The rooms are decorated with lots of items of china. The gardens include several country house conceits; a game larder, mechanical stile, and a coach-house, as well as the essential croquet and tennis facilities.

THE NORTH WEST AND THE LAKES

The Lungs of Manchester

The Lake District has long been nicknamed the 'lungs of Manchester'. Now the breath of fresh air supplied by its fells, lakes, and sheep pastures are easily reached via the M6 motorway spearing north from Chester.

Chester acts as a pleasant gateway to the area. The black and white timbered buildings and the Roman wall, around which the visitor can walk, make the city most appealing. It also offers excellent shopping, especially for fashions and antiques, in the 'rows': galleries of tiny shops, built for ease of locking and guarding in medieval times.

After the cloistered commerce of Chester, the Lakeland area comes as a contrast. The villages are small and hug the lakesides. The pace of life slows down – inevitably, as the roads around and between the thirteen lakes are narrow and, in season, full of tourist cars and buses. Its crowding is not new. In 1788 Wilberforce noted: 'The banks of the Thames are scarcely more public than those of Windemere.' Here feet are the best method of locomotion, starting out from a comfortable hotel base; or in summer you can take a trip on one of the old-style lake steamers and there is a steamboat museum at Bowness. Walkers can follow Roman tracks to the high fells; take on Helvellyn or the Langdale pikes; or climb the road from Troutbeck to Kirkstone for refreshment at the pub there, 1500 feet above sea level. There's no excuse not to try, at least. Especially considering the example set in the eighteenth century by Josiah Wedgwood, who went on walking holidays in the Lakes after having his leg amputated.

The Lake District National Park owes much to Beatrix Potter, who on her death in 1943 left four thousand acres to the nation, helping to establish it. Her farmhouse home at Near Sawrey on Ambleside is now owned by the National Trust, together with the nearby Tower Bank Arms, a small pub featured in *Jemima Puddleduck*, which serves local ales and comforting regional food. But the writer whose spirit towers over the Lakes is William Wordsworth. His homes, Dove Cottage and Rydal Mount, can both be visited; other houses which he either owned or had strong associations with, such as White Moss and Lancrigg, can be stayed in. His 'host of golden daffodils' can be seen around the lake edges in spring. At Kendal the Abbot Hall museum records traditional life styles both of the wealthy and rustic.

The Lakes have not only inspired poets, but cooks of the highest order. Outstanding examples are Francis Coulson at Sharrow Bay and John Tovey at Miller Howe, who writes cook-

Previous pages: Miller Howe provides superb views of the Lake District.

ery books and presents television programmes which are wonderfully evocative of the atmosphere of the Lakes.

At first glance Rookery Hall is very siimilar, architecturally, to its sister hotel Ettington Park. Built in the eighteenth century, Rookery Hall was bought in 1867 by one of Prince Albert's set, Baron William von Schroeder. He was the son of the founder of the great banking firm and became High Sheriff of Cheshire. He remodelled and extended the hall, adding a tower and putting in walnut, mahogany and chestnut panelling, a new main staircase in oak, and original Tudor oak panels in the Red room. The 28 acres of parkland stretch down to the River Weaver, and guests can try croquet, putting and tennis. The hotel has recently acquired a further two hundred acres of farmland and is considering installing a championship golf course with its own club house.

The bedrooms are well furnished with antiques and modern comforts, and look out on parkland. A first-floor suite has a William IV four-poster in which Mrs Thatcher once slept. There is fine china everywhere, and the rooms are named after the months of the year. 'May' has a canopied bed and Staffordshire china dogs for decoration. Its little bathroom has a tented, curtained bath. New arrivals find fruit, mint toffees, flowers and a personalized half-bottle of champagne placed in their rooms to welcome them.

After being greeted by a pin-striped butler, guests can relax in the long drawing room. This

Rookery Hall was built by a German banker friend of Prince Albert.

Rookery Hall
Worleston, near Nantwich, Cheshire CW5 6DQ
☎ (0270) 626866
Proprietors: Select Country Hotels. Member of Prestige.
Price grid A (includes dinner)

Location: Leave the M6 at Exit 16 and take the A560 to Nantwich; follow signs to Nantwich; after the railway crossing turn right at roundabout, following A51 signs to Chester; go through two sets of traffic lights and then turn right on to the B5074 to Winsford; Rookery Hall is 1½ miles on right before Worleston.
By rail to Crewe (6½ miles) and taxi. Helicopter pad.

runs the entire depth of the house, and in the corner it has a baroque German stove with elaborate decoration in pink, white and burgundy. Big chairs and sofas surround walnut inlaid tables under a moulded ceiling. The panelled dining room has another, more elaborate moulded ceiling. Here you can enjoy the seasonal menus produced by the chef, who used to cook at the Dorchester. His specialities include Cheshire cheese sausages served with Bramley apple and onion sauce; terrine of Whitby crab with mustard herb sauce; stew of duckling and pear lightly flavoured with ginger; hotchpotch of guinea fowl with herb dumplings; and glazed omelette of smoked haddock. Country warmers sprinkle the menus: oxtail and lentil broth with herb dumplings, mulled claret water ice, Lancashire duckling with apple prune and sage sauce, and bread-and-butter pudding with honey ice-cream.

Although Crabwall Manor is near enough to Chester to be able to see the cathedral spire from some of the rooms, the manor has 11 acres of gardens and fields, including a croquet lawn. As you approach the house, it looks quite modern, like a film set castle, but the history of the manor goes back a long way. In the 1080s, at the time of the Domesday Book, it was seized by William I's chief huntsman, the first Earl of Chester and founder of the Grosvenor dynasty. Later owners included a mayor of Chester, who is believed to have founded the city's mystery plays and who gave Crabwall to the church in return for prayers for his soul. A new house was built in Tudor times, but in the early nineteenth century the Tudor house was itself replaced by the present Grade II, listed building. This nevertheless has a Tudor Gothic castellated front, which affords some fine wrap-around room balconies.

Inside the glassed-in entrance below the clock tower and past a discreet reception area is a massive hall-cum-sitting room. Here there is plenty of pastel shaded seating and a huge stone walk-around fireplace with an inglenook and a staircase that curls round the back and leads to the bedrooms. In the two-level dining room Michael Truelove, who was formerly head chef at the *Michelin*-starred Box Tree in Ilkley and has been joined here by his award-winning kitchen team, presents a roast on a silver trolley every day, and interesting sauces with main course dishes: notably beetroot with guinea fowl, and ginger with angler fish fillets. Helpings are generous, for in Cheshire they like their food in larger quantities than are now normal. Free-range poultry is used, and,

Crabwall Manor
Mollington, Chester, Cheshire CH1 6NE
☎ (0244 851) 666
Directors: Carl Lewis and David Brockett. Member Prestige and Relais du Silence.
Price grid B
Notes: No children under 5 years; no dogs.

Location: 2 miles from centre of Chester. From Chester take the A540 towards West Kirby along Parkgate Road and the manor is on the left before the A5117 crossroads. Coming from the M56, take left turn, where the M56 ends, on to the A5717; turn left at the A540, and Crabwall Manor is on the right, 2 miles.
By rail to Chester General. Helicopter pad.

The modern entrance to Crabwell Manor.

wherever possible, organically grown produce. Vegetarian dishes will be served on request. There is an extensive wine list with 375 wines.

Crabwall is run by David Brockett, who was previously general manager at Chewton Glen. The overall design of the 26 bedrooms is Georgian, but each is individually styled. Some have open fires and balconies. A breakfast table and chairs are provided, as well as easy chairs, and most rooms have writing desks. The bathrooms have plants, telephones and two wash-basins. All have French-style wardrobes with glass doors lined with fabric. Six rooms are thoughtfully fitted with dual voltage sockets so that American guests can plug 110-volt appliances straight in. On the larger beds there are individual eiderdowns. There is a bedroom for disabled visitors, and in the clock tower the Ranulphus suite occupies the whole of the area, with a connecting bathroom between the sitting room and the bedroom doubling as a day meeting-room.

Crabwell Manor is tranquilly set though only a few minutes from Chester.

Many people shoot past the bulge of land on which Cartmel stands, an 800-year-old priory site in a traditional small village. The priory is one of the few to survive the Reformation, and still serves the community. Uplands has a serene setting in fields above the village and is reached up a steep and very narrow lane. Trees overhang the lane, which is typical of the area with its banks full of wild flowers.

The modest house, built by an admiral at the turn of the century, enjoys views over two acres of garden out to Morecambe Bay estuary. Tom Peter was one of John Tovey's head chefs at Miller Howe, and his wife Di was personal assistant to Tovey, who helped them set up their own small country hotel 'in the Miller Howe manner'. There are only four bedrooms, all double with shower rooms (one has a bathroom) and furnished with quilts on the beds and matching curtains, televisions, phones, hair-driers, clocks, Travel Scrabble and a supply of books. The ground floor has a colour scheme of pink, grey and blue, and the walls are hung with prints from the Metropolitan Museum of Art in New York.

Tom's meals are good value, and the dining room soon fills up. Particularly prized are the window tables looking out over the garden and valley. Tom's dishes include generous tureens of fennel and almond soup, served with hot wholemeal bread; and roast marinaded local wood pigeon, which comes on a pear purée with lemon thyme sauce. Desserts are a delight: apple and raspberry farmhouse pie with cream, Uplands tipsy trifle, or fresh cherries in amaretto cream in a white chocolate cup. But as at Miller Howe it is the selections and mixes of vegetables that are palate memories; mange-tout in hazelnut oil, carrots glazed with lemon or puréed with horseradish or white turnip in honey.

Miller Howe

Windermere, Cumbria
☎ (096 62) 2536
Owner: John Tovey
Price grid A (includes dinner)
Notes: Closed at beginning of the year

Location: Leave the M6 at Exit 36 and take the A590; just left of where A591 joins it, after Windermere village, Miller Howe is signed and set back from the road on a rise.

Miller Howe, with its gardens plunging downhill to steep pasture and views of Windermere below, has a Lutyens order on it for roof and chimney built in 1916 but is not a distinguished or historic house. Its delights stem from John Tovey, who in the early 1970s opened Miller Howe as a hotel and created here a magnet for food lovers. Tovey is not a classically trained chef; he worked in repertory theatre and, being short of money, learned to cook cheap ingredients well. He gained his first professional experience in Lake District hotels before opening his own restaurant at the Windermere Hydro, called Tonight at 8.30, and later, with the help of only three staff, Miller Howe.

Dinner at Miller Howe – lunch is not served – is still theatre. The staff work together like a well practised troupe. Guests must be at table on time for the 'curtain up' of the set meal, and Tovey goes round the tables introducing and discussing the courses. He admits that many of his ideas are made up as he goes along and that now, when an idea comes to him at home, he puts it straight on to his word-processor. He has also done much good work promoting British food abroad, as well as writing several cookery books and putting on a recent television series. Those who want to learn more at first hand can attend one of the cookery

Uplands Country House Hotel

Haggs Lane, Cartmel, Cumbria
☎ (05395) 36248/9
Owners: Tom and Diana Peter
Price grid B (includes dinner)
Notes: Closed after New Year for January and February. No children under 12 years.

Location From the M6 take Exit 36 towards Grange over Sands; turn left on to the A590, and go past Newby Bridge and across narrow lanes to Cartmel. With the Pig and Whistle pub on your right, turn left up Haggs Lane; Uplands is at the top of the hill on the left.

Uplands is an ex-Admiral's house now run in the Miller Howe style.

demonstrations he holds in the spring and autumn. Although set menus may deter some, a sample late spring menu shows the balance and variety he strives for, knowing that the flavours have to hold their own against the seductive backdrop of a late sunset over the hills: Miller Howe salad for a spring evening; parsnip and watercress soup with chilled diced apple; fillet of sea bass poached in yoghurt with fresh herb cream sauce and caviar tartlet; roast local guinea fowl on raspberry purée with bread sauce, prune and bacon roll and green peppercorn gravy. There is a choice of desserts, including warm orange syrup sponge pudding with Vanilla custard, squidgy chocolate rum gâteau, fudge and walnut slice, and deep fried dates stuffed with port and claret jelly. The same masterly treatment of vegetables as seen at Uplands is in evidence here: diced leeks in white wine, aubergine savoury casserole, cauliflower purée with toasted pine kernels, sliced courgettes cooked in Marsala are among the lively selection.

During the New Year closure period John Tovey spends time travelling, often bringing back more items to decorate the house. His eclectic collections of objects from his travels already flow into the bedrooms, which are named after the lakes.

A cherub in the grounds of Miller Howe.

Lindeth Fell is a superbly sited house, built in 1907 of solid Lakeland stone. Its magnificent gardens contain a private fishing tarn, croquet, tennis and putting green, and provide colour throughout the year. The gardens were planted with masses of bulbs, which bloom in spring, followed by azaleas and

Lindeth Fell, which is set in beautiful gardens, overlooks Lake Windermere.

rhododendrons, and later by roses; in autumn there are maples and pines to supply brilliant colours. The whole looks down to Lake Windermere, and the terrace-style dining room makes the most of the views.

It is a place where people come in from walks and settle down with guide-books, magazines and binoculars in the lounges filled with the souvenirs and pictures collected by Pat Kennedy, a retired air commodore. The fifteen bedrooms, which are named after the lakes, all have bathroom, colour television, tea-making facilities, guide-books, hair-drier.

Diana Kennedy presents *cordon bleu* style cooking, but also English puddings and a traditional Sunday lunch. A typical menu might include potted Morecambe Bay shrimps, baked cheese soufflé, salmon and parsley soup, sole fillets filled with prawns and asparagus sauce, Cumberland rum nicky, bread-and-butter pudding, and local English cheese. Kendal chocolate mint cake is served with the coffee.

Lindeth Fell
Country House Hotel,
Bowness on Windermere,
Cumbria LA23 3JP
☎ (09662) 3286
Owners: Pat and Diana Kennedy
Price grid C (includes dinner)
Notes: Closed November to March

Location: Take A591 from Windermere to Bowness; continue through Bowness and take the A5074; just after it crosses the B5284 road. Lindeth Fell is off to the left, up a steep drive.

This is one of the most peaceful and welcoming of small country house hotels. It has an almost cottagey feel, with flowers climbing the grey stone walls, parts of which date from 1730. By a tiny slate-covered porch there is a small flagged patio where one can take coffee and drinks at the very spot where William Wordsworth sat and rested on his walks from Rydal to Grasmere. Wordsworth used to own the house, but he rented it out, only keeping it in order to be able to vote in Rydal against the railway coming through. Dorothy Wordsworth called the White Moss lands 'a fairy place', and the hotel keeps a folder of her walks and the maps she used to follow. In 1802 Dorothy Wordsworth wrote: 'this White Moss, a place made for all kinds of beautiful works of art and nature, woods and valleys, fairy valleys and fairy tarns, miniature mountains, alps, above alps'. There is National Trust land all around, but the hotel grounds, cut by walking tracks, climb steeply behind the house through wild flowers to Brockstone Cottage. Rented as a hotel room for those who really want to be away from it all, the cottage is high up in superb country for walking and for watching deer.

White Moss House has five bedrooms. Each is equipped with thoughtful details; a bag of sewing needs to match the curtains, hair-dryer, trouser press, television and radio, toiletries, maps, guides, books and fresh flowers. The old part of the house was once three cottages. Some of the beds are covered in lace, others in floral fabrics. Flowers are a White Moss theme, and even the menus are decorated with robins,

White Moss House
Rydal Water, Grasmere,
Cumbria LA22 9SE
☎ (096 65) 295
Owners: Peter and Sue Dixon
Price grid B (includes dinner)
Note: Closed November to mid-March

Location: On the A591 Windermere to Grasmere road. White Moss is set on right-hand side (going north) of the road opposite Rydal Water.

White Moss was once owned by William Wordsworth.

rabbits, tall foxgloves and other wild flowers.

Peter Dixon prepares the daily menu and looks after the wines from a remarkably large selection of 200 bins. Guests are invited for dinner at 7.30 for 8 (not on Sundays). Dishes in spring might include courgette and rosemary soup, and Lakeland chicken breast poached in old yellow Jura wine, with fresh herb and lime pâté and tarragon and saffron sauce. Rydal pike, which can weigh over twenty pounds, is souffléd with dill, and is especially good because of the clear water in which it lives. Puddings are old favourites: Mrs Beeton's chocolate pudding, Kentish Well pudding with its well of lemon sauce inside a suet crust, Cabinet pudding (so rarely seen today) with fluffy lemon sabayon sauce.

The Dixons have collected together an amazing array of English cheeses, so many in fact that they are listed separately. Among them are Coleford Blue, made from ewe's milk, Wackley, a soft ewe's milk cheese, Smoked Cumberland farmhouse, Cloisters, made to a thirteenth-century monastic recipe; Blackwood Moorlands goat cheese, a mould-ripened cheese; Alston Tynedale, and Satterleigh, an organic goats' cheese from Devon. The breakfast fare is hearty and flavourful too: natural yoghurt and fresh juices, followed by the White Moss platter of bacon, fried egg, Cumberland sausage, tomato, mushroom, black pudding and fried bread.

'**U**pon a forest side at Grasmere Vale/ There dwelt a shepherd. Michael was his name . . .' So wrote Wordsworth in 'Michael', which he composed at Dove Cottage in 1800. Michael's Nook got its name from this poem. The house was built of Lakeland stone from a now defunct local quarry in 1859. At the turn of the century a Rochdale industrialist added Honduras mahogany woodwork, plaster mouldings in the hall and drawing room, and, as the present owner says, 'impressive plumbing, still working well'.

The house was a family home until 1969, when Reg Gifford bought it. He retains its private feel; the doorbell must be rung for admittance at a conservatory-style entrance. There are no keys to the rooms, though each arriving guest finds a card bearing his or her name, the date and a little illustration of the bird after which the room is named. Gifford likes birds and encourages them in the garden; he also owns a parrot, whom he is training to greet guests, a Great Dane which already does, and two exotic long-haired cats.

Gifford previously had an antiques business, and Michael's Nook is filled with his collection of

Michael's Nook
Grasmere, Cumbria
LA22 9RP
☎ (09665) 496
Owner: Reg Gifford.
Member of Pride of Britain
Price grid A (includes dinner)

Location: Take the A591 to Grasmere, but do not turn left into the village; instead continue north on the A591 and turn right at the Old Swan hotel up to Michael's Nook.

English prints, rugs and porcelain. The bedrooms show the care that is taken over details; each has fruit, flowers, mineral water, an umbrella, Scrabble, books, and scales in the bathroom. 'Chaffinch' faces west, and its high wooden four-poster has antique steps for climbing on to it and antique bedside cupboards decorated with china. Bathrooms are big and white. Two suites have been created in an old hay loft with sitting room, private patio and little garden. The 'best' suite is 'Owl', which is on two levels, linked by a spiral staircase, and has a terrace with a view of the valley. The lace curtains were made in Scotland, and a superb chinese wardrobe and bed set dating from the 1890s forms the decor nucleus. Beds are made while guests are at breakfast; a house rule that makes a very good impression on guests when they return from the dining room.

Dinner menus are placed in the bedrooms; guests inform reception of their choices in advance, to make dinner service smoother. Reg Gifford likes to escort his guests into dinner on time, and the food is superb enough to make the punctuality worthwhile. Chef Harry Nagler trained with Peter Kromberg at the Intercontinental in London, and his specialities include a starter of whole quail, filled with *foie gras*, in flaky pastry with red wine and truffle sauce; sweet potato and garlic soup; freshly baked lobster tail in Dover sole fillets with light butter vanilla sauce; chocolate truffle cake, hot apple and cinnamon parcels and summer pudding with blackcurrant coulis. Alternatives are given in addition to the 'chef's suggestion', and there is always fresh orange juice available.

Michael's Nook was named after a character in one of Wordsworth's poems who was said to have lived here.

Window glass at Lancrigg.

Lancrigg is an appealing whitewashed house, set snugly in woods beneath the hump of a fell. The terraced gardens are edged with beech hedges and well supplied with toys belonging to the Whittington children. (Lancrigg lays on earlier meals for children.) The hotel is in the centre of the Lake District National Park and there are good walks starting right at the door.

Lancrigg is an early seventeenth-century farmhouse (its period barns next door may become a tea-room), which was enlarged in the 1850s. The rounded Lakeland chimneys were specified by Wordsworth in his capacity as agent for a friend who was buying the house. The poet was a regular visitor, along with Samuel Taylor Coleridge, Tennyson and De Quincey. The grounds were a favourite haunt of William and Dorothy – a Latin plaque in the woods commemorates their visits – and William wrote the major part of *The Prelude* here. In the 1860s Lancrigg was the house of Sir John Booth Richardson, a friend of Darwin and Huxley, and a surgeon on Arctic explorations. He landscaped the woods, which contain many specimen trees. In spring the 27 acres are bright with azaleas and rhododendrons.

After a wintry walk along the beck or following Wordsworth's trails, the log fires in the drawing and dining rooms are very welcoming. Not all the ten bedrooms have private bathrooms (four do), but the suites have four-poster beds draped with lace, whirlpool baths and private outside sitting areas. Floral duvets and wallpapers enhance the rural atmos-

Lancrigg Vegetarian Country House Hotel
Easedale, Grasmere, Cumbria LA22 9QN
☎ (09665) 317
Owners: Robert and Janet Whittington
Price grid C
Note: Closed from mid January and February

Location: Take the A591 to Grasmere; at Dove Cottage turn left into the village; at the bookshop follow the Easedale road, a narrowing path full of walkers from the Youth hostel; by the footpath to Easedale turn into Lancrigg drive.

phere, echoed also in the vegetarian food. Organic local produce is used, as well as free-range eggs and vegetarian cheese, and the gardens are being developed to provide fresh fruit, vegetables and herbs. The wine list includes fruit wines and organic French wines. Robert Whittington does the cooking, and in addition to fresh soups, dishes include chick pea and tarragon casserole, with rice and salad; traditional lemon pudding, and home-made ice-creams. The breakfast menu is a buffet of pure fruit juices, fresh fruit salad or stewed fruits, muesli with fresh or soya milk, scrambled eggs, buckwheat pancakes with savoury mushroom filling, and wholemeal toast.

Sharrow Bay has been given many awards; among them that of having the best restaurant view in Britain. The house was built in 1840 and is not very distinguished architecturally, though it would in any case be difficult to rival the lake views. It remained a private house until Francis Coulson opened it as a hotel in 1949. Brian Sack joined soon after, and they became the pioneers of country house hotels as places where food and service are as important as comfortable bedrooms. At the beginning they ran it as a kind of ex-service men's commune. Nowadays the rooms are supplied with down pillows and Percale sheets with embroidered edges, toiletries, china, biscuit barrels by the bed, and furnished with English antique furniture and the owners' collections of ornaments. The rooms vary: some have no bathroom, and cost a little less; some have balconies. There are 22 bedrooms in the main house, and a cottage in the grounds containing two suites with two bedrooms each, and a separate bedroom with its own private entrance. The Edwardian lodge by the gates has more rooms; and four miles away is a seventeenth-century cottage with two bedrooms, a sitting room, a small kitchen and a sun room. The cottage is serviced by hotel staff, and meals are taken at Sharrow. Bank House, situated by the lake one mile from Sharrow, has a wonderful refectory dining room

Sharrow Bay
Lake Ullswater, Penrith, Cumbria CA10 2LZ
☎ (08536) 301/483
Owners: Francis Coulson and Brian Sack. Member of Relais et Châteaux
Price grid A+ (includes dinner)
Note: Closed early December to beginning of March

Location: Leave the M6 at Exit 40; take the A66 towards Keswick; turn left on to the A592 to Patterdale, then right to Pooleybridge; go through the village, follow the road round the top of Ullswater towards Howtown; and Sharrow Bay is signed on the right of this road.

The garden at Sharrow Bay.

in a converted barn, with a fireplace from Warwick Castle, tapestry chairs from Parham House and a vaulted beamed ceiling. Here guests are served a full English breakfast, morning coffee and afternoon tea. Rooms here are named after the heroines of *Herries Chronicle*, Hugh Walpole's series of novels set in the Lakes. One heroine, Deborah, slept with all; her room is therefore downstairs in case anyone wants to come in discreetly.

In the main house, in addition to two drawing rooms, there is a recently added conservatory and two dining rooms with little alcoves for privacy. At one end there is a hidden, alpine-style balcony, which makes a good hideaway spot for after-lunch coffee and offers a stunning view down the lake to the Martindale fells, with steamers and other boats passing below. Guests can sail or fish – or just walk off yet another superb meal. Coulson's staff have instructions to offer refreshments whenever guests arrive, and cards are kept detailing guests' likes and dislikes.

The single-sheet menu lists all the chefs and the restaurant manager by name, and the page is packed with goodies. However, it seems that if you leave the choice to Francis Coulson he will unerringly pick just the kind of meal you are in the mood for. On Sundays there is a 'traditional lunch' with lots of meats, poultry and game roasts, omelettes, and a cold table with ox tongue and Cumberland ham. Among the puddings – and the dessert trolley is shown to guests as they go to their table – are Sticky Toffee sponge (a steamed syrup sponge with creamy egg custard), which has been much copied, Coeur à la crème with strawberries, strawberry hazelnut and meringue gâteau, chocolate brandy cake, apple and almond brulée, gratinated summer fruit, and walnut tart with lime sauce.

Farlam Hall dates from the late seventeenth century. John Wesley is reputed to have preached in the house, and George Stephenson of steam engine fame stayed there. His 'Rocket' belonged to the family who lived at Farlam, and spent the last years of its working life on the local line that at one time ran through the gardens on a special track. The house was enlarged to its present size in Victorian times by a rich coal and mineral magnate with two private mines.

The interior is still very Victorian, with many period antiques; Victorian dolls and silver line shelves in the main corridor. The sitting room with its open fire and big bay window was once the billiards room. The dining room has curtains to divide it and deep blue decor; it

Farlam Hall
Brampton,
Cumbria CA8 2NG
☎ (06976) 234
Owners: The Quinion family. Member of Relais et Châteaux
Price grid B (includes dinner)
Notes: Closed February, No children under 5 years. Dogs by prior arrangement (and only one per bedroom, not to be left alone)

Location: Take the M6 north towards Carlisle; leave the motorway at Exit 43 and take the A69 to Brampton and then the A689 towards Hallbankgate; Farlam Hall is on the left-hand side, 2½ miles from Brampton.

Victorian dolls among the decoration in Farlam's public rooms.

overlooks the gardens that descend to a stream, pond and waterfall, popular with wild birds. Croquet is also available. There is a small bar by the entrance hall.

There are thirteen bedrooms opening off a long corridor. The spacious rooms have floral fabrics and coloured ceilings and wallpaper. The garden room on the ground floor has a six-foot four-poster.

Farlam Hall is well sited as a stop-over on the way to or from Scotland. The surrounding area around is little known but well worth exploring. Indeed, the best parts of Hadrian's Wall start just four miles away, including the latest dig, reckoned to be the most important in Cumbria to date. The Solway coast, Scottish borders, Northumberland and Lake District are all within easy reach.

Barry Quinion is in charge of the kitchen (his sister Helen runs the hotel), and the menu is changed nightly. His aim is to achieve the right balance between light presentation and sustaining food for those who have been out in the brisk air all day. Dinner is served at 8 p.m. (orders placed by 7.30 p.m.), and there is a choice of courses. A starter can be cream of radish soup, pancake of spinach and nutmeg, dariole of seafood on dill cream sauce, or hot tart of smoked salmon and prawns. On Saturday nights a sorbet is served before the main course, which might be Galloway lobster with mushrooms, chicken breast filled with spinach and walnuts with fresh herb sauce, or fillet of halibut with fresh spinach in filo pastry with lobster sauce.

THE NORTH EAST

The Texas of Britain

Yorkshire, they say – and Yorkshire people do speak up for themselves – has as many acres as there are letters in the Bible. Recent boundary reorganizations may have diluted that, but it is still Britain's biggest county. Yorkshire is the Texas of England, where everything is just that little bit bigger; even the food portions. A 26oz steak is quite normal, followed by apple pie and cheese – 'a piece of pie without the cheese, is like a kiss without the squeeze'. The Barnsley chop, where a saddle of lamb is cut lengthwise to provide a double chop, shows true Yorkshire dimensions in its standard portions: 4½lb uncooked meat for men and 3¼lb for women (the county is also fairly chauvinistic).

Denby Dale, near Barnsley, was the home of giant pies which required engineering know-how to build ovens big enough to cook them. The first pie was baked in 1788 to celebrate King George III's recovery from illness; thereafter giant pies became the local way of commemorating historic events, though now they are used more frequently for fund-raising purposes. The 1846 pie, baked in the euphoria following the repeal of the Corn Laws, was 21 feet across and contained a medley of meats. The 1964 pie, slimmer at 18 by 6 feet, was used to raise money for a village hall, now known as Pie Hall. In 1988 two hundred years of pie pride were marked with another great pie. The biggest banquet ever recorded in Britain was held in the fifteenth century at Cawood, west of Leeds, when five hundred deer and a thousand oxen were prepared by two thousand cooks.

It is not therefore surprising that *nouvelle cuisine* didn't go down favourably in the north-east. It is a region where they like to go out to eat, particularly at weekends, but they like value for money and honest portions, 'not messed about' – traditional favourites such as Yorkshire pudding, roast beef, fish and chips are still going strong. With the brisk winds that blow in off the North Sea – Scarborough has been described euphemistically as the most 'bracing' of resorts – hearty appetites are soon built up.

The same applies as one moves northwards through Cleveland and Northumberland towards the Borders, that wild warring country of the past.

The moors and dales are exhilarating areas to explore. Here there is good rock-climbing and famous long walks like the Lyke Wake walk from Osmotherley in North Yorkshire to Ravenscar.

More shelter is provided in the hidden dales like Dentdale where once everyone – man, woman and child – used to knit in every spare

Previous pages: Linden Hall, Northumberland.

moment, on the move or round peat fires in the evenings. Dentdale has Britain's national caving centre and underground caverns as big as several double-decker buses. The coast of the north-east is magnificent but tough. Grace Darling, the lighthouse-keeper's daughter who rowed through a storm to rescue passengers from a shipwreck is a local heroine; and Captain James Cook grew up in Whitby, learning seamanship in a Whitby collier. The raw wind blowing here at Easter, when custard dishes were traditionally baked, was known as 'the custard wind'.

In contrast with the wildness and windiness of its scenery, the north-east has a wealth of ecclesiastical buildings and cosy, often walled, towns. At York you can walk round the walls and admire the medieval cobbled streets with their Viking-derived names. Nearby Beverley has its minster, too, with humourous and superbly carved misericord seats. Ripon has another mighty cathedral, with delightfully carved fifteenth-century choir stalls on which two pigs can be seen dancing to a bagpipe played by a third, and a mermaid holding a mirror and a brush. Today the hornblower still sounds the Wakeman's hour at dusk to warn of the dangers of the night, as he has done since Saxon times. Many of the abbeys and monastic buildings since Reformation days are elegant ruins: notably Jervaulx Abbey, Fountains Abbey, Rievaulx Abbey, where they could feed 740 people back in the thirteenth century, Guisborough Priory and Byland Abbey. In Northumberland the Bede monastery at Jarrow has a church with the only Saxon stained glass in the world, and a museum telling the story of Saxon Northumberland's monastic life. After the monasteries died, the tradition of hospitality may have faded a little; now, however, more and more of the somewhat stern manors and houses of the area are being opened as hotels, characterized by sensible prices and a motherly welcome.

Situated just west of the Northumberland border, Lovelady Shield has probably the wildest surroundings of any hotel in this book. Roads going south from here lead over the high unpeopled moors, past Middleton in Teesdale and Barnard Castle, and eventually down to Wensleydale. Alston is England's highest market town, and all around are the rolling fells of the High Pennines, which can be seen from the road, a roller-coaster of dips and highs in purpling browns and greens, where the hills are worn smooth by age. It is a place for the energetic. One can play croquet on the neat lawn behind Lovelady Shield house; there is

Lovelady Shield Country House Hotel
Alston, Cumbria CA9 3LF
☎ (0498) 81203
Owners: Barry and Annie Rosier
Price grid C
Notes Closed in January. Dogs by prior arrangement

Location Take the A689 from Carlisle and Brampton to Alston; continue through Alston; after 2½ miles, before you reach Nenthead, Lovelady Shield is set back from the road in trees on the left.

also tennis, and golf nearby, but sports more in keeping with the surroundings are fishing, shooting and riding. Above all, this is walking country, with the Pennine Way passing through Alston, and Hadrian's Wall half an hour away.

The hotel, at the end of a long, tree-lined drive, is secluded but has splendid views. Once a nunnery, it has been a farm since 1587, and the present house dates from about 1830. The origin of its enchanting name is a little obscure, although we know that 'shield' comes from 'shieling', meaning summer house or shelter. The house is shielded by wooded hillside, and the River Nent runs along the other side of the two-acre gardens, forming, as Barry Rosier puts it, 'an oasis of ordered tranquillity among the wild and rolling fells'.

The small cosy rooms are warm, too, with open fires underscored by central heating. There is a small library crammed with books, a drawing room where a log fire burns most of the year, and a patio off it where on sunny days one can sit beneath the martins' nests under the eaves. The twelve bedrooms all have private bathroom, or shower and toilet; the beds have electric blankets; and facilities include direct dial phone, colour television, radio and hairdrier; drying and ironing facilities are available. The rooms have pine doors, and floral wallpapers and duvets give them a cottagey feel. A little bar is set in the former dining room, and what is now the dining room, with its pink decor and red chairs, looks out on the croquet lawn. Food is local produce but with French input from French born Annie. The six-course dinner will satisfy the hungriest walker or fisherman. There is a choice of half a dozen starters, cream

The cosy interiors of Lovelady Shield Hotel are a contrast to the wild moorland outside.

of Jerusalem artichoke soup with lemon croutons; a main course perhaps best end of lamb with herb crust and mild garlic and white wine sauce, or fillet of salmon topped with pike mousseline baked in a filo pastry and served with a watercress and champagne sauce; each comes with a platter of assorted vegetables; and finally a choice of cold desserts is served with local Jersey cream. The English cheeseboard includes Cotherstone from Barnard Castle and smoked Tynedale from Alston Moor. Though remote, the wine list is varied and large (a hundred are listed), including Australian and New Zealand vintages. Vegetarian meals can be served if notice is given. Lunch is only served on Sundays, when there is traditional fare such as roast beef and Yorkshire pudding, steak and kidney pudding and chicken curry. The inclusive breakfast will keep most going until dinner. As well as juice and cereals, there is porridge, stewed fruit compote, natural yoghurt from the Cathwaite pedigree local Jersey herd, a choice of egg dishes, grilled bacon, Cumberland sausage with tomato and fried bread, and – as available – mushrooms with lamb's kidneys, grilled Loch Fyne kippers or kedgeree.

Linden Hall was built by a local merchant banker and high sheriff of Northumberland in 1812 on part of a 2,000-acre estate purchased from the Earl of Carlisle. The house, which takes its name from a nearby river, was designed by Sir Charles Monck and John Dobson, and built in local stone. Later additions include the white marble Adam fireplace in the bar. In 1978 the house and a 300-acre estate was bought by the century-old Callers-Pegasus Travel Service, who have restored the listed building in Georgian style, preserving the Tuscan portico, staircase and lantern and the classical mouldings of the rooms. It now has 45 bedrooms, used mainly by conference delegates during the week and family and leisure visitors at weekends. The stable courtyard has been made into conference suites and banqueting rooms, and in 1988 the hall won an RIBA architectural award. In addition to the individual and antique bedrooms in the main house, there are two cottages, Holly Cottage and The Bothy, in its private walled courtyard.

The Dobson Room restaurant, with its green moulded ceiling and Regency striped walls overlooks the croquet lawn and formal gardens. Dinner is served by candlelight, with piano accompaniment and flowers for the ladies. A more relaxing place to eat is the Linden Pub in an old granary adjoining the hotel. This has natural exposed stone walls and a collection of

Linden Hall Hotel
Longhorsley, Morpeth, Northumberland
☎ (0670) 516611
Proprietors: Callers-Pegasus Travel Service. Member of Prestige
Price grid B

Location: A1(M) north through Gateshead and Newcastle to Morpeth; take the A697 to Longhorsley and go through the village; Linden Hall is on the right 1 mile after the village.
By rail to Newcastle; ferries from Scandinavia to Newcastle. Helicopter pad.

old advertising signs. It serves North Country fare, and in fine weather the courtyard outside is used for outdoor draughts and boules.

Wensleydale is Herriott country, and Hawes a popular tourist centre. Rookhurst is about half a mile from the centre of Hawes and has the advantage of being set within a charming village of stone houses with bright small gardens. From Gayle one can go up to Fleet Moss; tour the moors to Kettlewell; see Malham Cove and Gordale Scar, Aysgarth Falls, Cotterforce and Hardraw Force, the highest single-drop fall in England which made a deep impression on Wordsworth. Distance walking, fishing, sailing, canoeing, pot-holing, hang-gliding and pony trekking are all popular local activities.

Rookhurst's new owner, Iris Van der Steen, comes from the London area but has fallen in love with Gayle and Wensleydale. She is not the first southern owner. Although the house dates originally from the seventeenth century, most of it was built in the 1860s, when the owner was a London barrister. The Victorian Gothic exterior is well echoed by period furnishings inside, where the level of comfort is very high in relation to the room prices. There are five bedrooms with their own bathroom. The master bedroom has a walnut 1770 four-poster. The beamed (1620) bridal suite runs the length of the Georgian farmhouse section of the house; it has a half-tester bed, a dining area and a bathroom with original Royal Doulton fittings. The half-acre garden is pleasant for sitting out and enjoying the peaceful views.

The dinner menu, which changes daily, is not long, but four vegetables are offered with the main course. The owners go round with the menu at about 6 pm, taking orders from the choice of four items in each course. Specialities include cream of broccoli and Wensleydale cheese soup, pasta shells stuffed with fresh salmon mousse, roast lamb, veal escalopes in cream and mushroom sauce, chocolate fudge cake, and bananas in rum sauce.

Up on a ridge of hills overlooking Hawes and Wensleydale to the south is Simonstone Hall. It has lovely terraced gardens and superb views, which can be enjoyed over a bar lunch, perhaps after coming in from a walk above the valley – best explored from this side. The hall was once the home of the Earls of Wharncliffe and dates mainly from 1733 (one places in the drawing rooms have peacock mouldings over them, which were rescued in 1884 from the burnt-out ruins of Belmont Castle. Paintings and tapestries, books and

A detail from the staircase at Rookhurst.

Rookhurst
Gayle, Hawes, North Yorkshire DL8 3RT
☎ (09697) 454
Owners: Mr and Mrs Van der Steen
Price grid C (includes dinners)
Notes: Closed from 15 December to the end of January. No children or pets.

Location: Taking the A684 (25 miles away from M6) Sedburgh exit to Hawes; in Hawes turn right to Gayle; turn right in Gayle through a narrow street and Rookhurst is signed on the right.

The stained-glass stair window at Simonstone Hall.

coats of arms of the Earls abound. Above the main staircase, with its high stained-glass windows, hangs a portrait of Lady Mary Wortley Montagu, painted by Kneller. Lady Mary (see also Middlethorpe Hall on page 165) inherited the house in 1755 and made it her home. She was an intrepid early traveller and was one of the first to be immunized against smallpox. The bar, with old church panelling, stained glass and pew style alcoves, serves lunches daily, whilst after dinner coffee is served in the adjacent panelled drawing room. The ten bedrooms, many of which are large, all have private bathroom (one has a shower room), televisions and tea-makers. One has a four-poster draped with Laura Ashley fabric and piled with heart-shaped scented cushions.

The well-preserved Georgian dining room, white panelling with original portraits, some from the Jeffryes family. Candles, silver, crystal glasses and Wedgwood china go well with the room. On the menu there are dishes to delight the walker: cream of Wensleydale soup and roast loin of pork with apple sauce.

Jervaulx Hall was built in 1856 of golden stone, has a courtyard garden at the front and a side garden leading to Jervaulx Abbey, which was founded in 1156. Now its ruined walls are covered with marjoram and wallflowers, and over 120 species of wild flower have been recorded in the grounds. It was here that the monks first made Wensleydale cheese, originally from ewe's milk.

The Hall's gardens are sheltered by tree covered rising ground to the north and the main lawn on the south side leads towards the abbey

Simonstone Hall
Hawes, North Yorkshire
DL8 3LY
☎ (09697) 255
Owners: John and Sheila Jeffryes
Price grid C
Note: Dogs welcome and allowed in bedrooms; a small charge is made.

Location: (to reach Hawes see above). Go through Hawes and turn left (going east) following signs to Simonstone and Muker; follow signs at T-junction climbing hill and hotel is signed on left.

and its park. One bedroom on the ground floor, with its own doorway opening on to the eight-acre garden, is ideal for the elderly, disabled or guests with dogs.

The entrance hall is big and delightfully furnished with antiques and paintings. It leads to a formal drawing room with piano, chandeliers and many more antiques. When the weather is chilly there are cheering log fires in the two reception rooms. There is no bar, but guests are asked to help themselves and use the honesty book. The eight bedrooms all have bathrooms and tea-making facilities, and are furnished in soft colours.

Dinner is at 8 p.m., and guests place their orders thirty minutes in advance. *Hors d'oeuvres* might be pear stuffed with tarragon cream or smoked mackerel quiche; typical main courses are steak and kidney pie, pork chops with tomato and mustard cream sauce, and trout in green ginger wine with almonds; and desserts include banana chartreuse, fresh fruit Pavlova and *crème brûlée*.

Jervaulx Hall
Ripon, North Yorkshire
☎ (0677) 60235
Owner: John Sharp
Price grid B (includes dinner)
Notes: Closed mid-November to March (except for parties of eight or more). Dogs by arrangement, but not left in bedrooms.

Location: On the A6108 4½ miles north of Masham and 5 miles south of Leyburn. The Hall is on the right side of the road, going north, immediately next to the ruins of Jervaulx Abbey. 20 minutes from the A1.

Wood Hall is set on a hill rise and has an imposing pillared portico and a solid square Georgian façade that recalls houses around Bath. It looks arrogantly down over a hundred acres of parkland to the little villages in the valley below. Behind the hotel lives an enclosed order of nuns.

The house was built in 1750 by 'Soapy Joe' Watson, a soap magnate who became the first Lord Manton. Since then it has served at various times as a preparatory school, a Roman Catholic retreat, a home for Vietnamese boat people and, since April 1988, a hotel. The interior is extremely grand. Pink carpeted stairs lead up to the 22 bedrooms, each of which has had about £60,000 spent on it. There is linen from Belgium and merino wool blankets from Huddersfield, and each guest is greeted with a four-inch tall Wood Hall teddy bear on the pillow. Six of the bedrooms are in a Jacobean-style wing built of old stone. Four-posters, half-testers, draped crowns over beds, clothed side tables, and gas 'coal' fires are characteristic features, together with rich fabrics in yellow butterfly or pink wild strawberry patterns. Bathroom decor and tile detail in each case is taken from the curtain fabric. One room has big beams across its centre and toy ducks in the bathroom.

Plenty of sports facilities are offered, and there are plans for a golf course. Croquet, hot-air ballooning and archery can be arranged, and a minibus takes guests to Leeds and Harrogate for shopping, for shooting on the moors, or on outings to Harewood House nearby.

Wood Hall
Linton, near Wetherby, West Yorkshire
☎ (0937) 67271
Proprietor: Select Country Hotels
Price grid B

Location: From Wetherby take the Harrogate road north from the market place for half a mile; turn left towards Sickling-hall and Linton, cross bridge and turn left, following signs to Linton and Wood Hall; follow road into Linton for 1 mile, passing Wetherby golf course on the left; turn right in middle of Linton opposite the Windmill pub and follow estate road through open farmland for 1¼ miles to the Hall. Leeds and Harrogate 15 minutes; York 20 minutes.
Helicopter pad.

The entrance to Jervaulx Hall.

The terrace at Wood Hall.

The public rooms are splendidly Georgian with big sofas round open fires off the lobby, paintings, noble floral displays, rugs, whatnots with plants, and china in shelved recesses. The dining room has Georgian striped wallpaper, and the tables are graced with crockery from Luxembourg and silver plate from Austria. The chef is Michael Riley from Inverlochy Castle, who has also worked at Gravetye, Hambleton Hall and for the American ambassador. A 'menu gastronomique' is available at 48 hours' notice. Specialities are smoked salmon lined with Nori seaweed and rolled in its own mousse, lightly curried whitebait soup and venison consommé with juniper, layered chocolate and Grand Marnier gâteau with a marmalade sauce, and grilled pineapple on wild rice pudding with a rum sabayon.

A resplendently dressed butler greets guests at this immaculate house. He escorts them to their rooms and provides any necessary information. The house dates back to the Domesday Book, and for seven hundred years belonged to the Fairfax family; it was they who built the present house in 1903, in place of a decaying Tudor building. The most famous Fairfax was Black Tom, creator and commander of Parliament's New Model Army that defeated Charles I. He appointed Andrew Marvell as tutor to his daughter Mary, and eventually helped restore Charles II to the throne. He is buried in the chapel at Bilbrough, which is now a conservation village.

The Bells bought Bilbrough in 1986 and set about installing a traditional style of country house hospitality. The reception hall with log fire is large and stately with arches leading through to a cocktail bar, and panelled rooms with big sofas, alcoves for china, and panelling. The twelve bedrooms are richly furnished with bright colours, open fireplaces, plenty of cushions and the four-poster beds and velvet tub chairs. There is 24-hour room service. The rooms bear maiden names of Fairfax wives, except for 'Fairfax' itself, which is the master

Bilbrough Manor
Bilbrough, York YO2 3PH
☎ (0937) 834002
Owners: Colin and Susan Bell
Price grid B
Notes: No children under 12 years; no pets.

Location: Off the A64 York/Leeds road take turning signed Bilbrough village to north of road; just before the village turn left to Bilbrough Manor.
By rail to York. Helicopter pad.

One of the bedrooms at Bilborough Manor.

bedroom, with mullioned windows, a pink four-poster, an enormous bathroom, and a sitting/dining area.

The oak panelled dining room has pink napery, silver cutlery, engraved glasses and ladderback chairs. Idris Caldora, the 1986 Young Chef of the Year, presents 'new classical French cooking'; his 'menu exceptionel' includes dishes like veal sweetbreads on celeriac and apple with Madeira sauce, and dark chocolate terrine with spiced Anglaise sauce. The wine list emphasizes French vintages, while the vegetables and herbs are home-grown. The Manor has four acres of gardens and a further hundred acres of farmland.

Although Middlethorpe is situated in the suburbs of York, overlooking the race-course area, the immediate surroundings are rural in character. Its 26 acres of gardens include a ha-ha, a lake, specimen trees, and walled gardens for herbs and flowers, where guests can buy plants to take home.

The William and Mary house was built in 1699-1701 of mellow red brick with limestone dressing. It was built conveniently, if curiously, close to the road by a rich master cutler with pretensions to be a country gent. With its north entrance front of seven bays and three full storeys, topped with an eagle, the cutler's family crest, the house is reminiscent of Hampton Court. Flanking wings were added at the end of the eighteenth century. The house was briefly the home of Lady Mary Wortley Montagu, who wrote that it was a 'very pritty place' (sic). In the 1970s it was allowed to decay, and for a while it was a somewhat unsalubrious disco.

The entrance leads directly to a black and white flagstone floor and a fine carved oak staircase, supported by pillars, with portraits hung above it. On one side are the dining rooms; on the other a library leads through to an impressive drawing room: formerly a ball-room, it has an elaborately moulded ceiling, fine portraits, striped or chintz-covered chairs and sofas, and heavy yellow brocade drapes. A beautiful cabinet at one end holds a collection of porcelain. Books, writing desks, and flowers give it a less than formal air. Middlethorpe exudes that period but live-in feel – as if Lady Mary had just left the room.

The dining room has fine panelling with carved Ionic pilasters. Fireplaces, paintings and views of the gardens complete the effect of dining in a private house. The former chef, Aiden McCormack, has joined Hartwell House (see page 29). His successor, Kevin Franksen, has kept the established recipe pattern such as

Middlethorpe Hall
Bishopthorpe Road, York
YO2 1QP
☎ (0904) 641241
Proprietors: Historic House Hotels
General Manager: Malcolm Broadbent. Member of Prestige
Price grid B
Notes: No children under 8 years; no dogs.

Location: Take the A64 going towards York, turn left to Tadcaster Road, A1036 past London Bridge petrol station; take the first right over the A64, first left, then first left again past the Archbishop's Palace on the right; Middlethorpe Hall is just after this on the right. 1½ miles York and railway station. (2 hours from London).

Middlethorpe Hall is a mellow, red brick and limestone William and Mary house.

rabbit and pear pâté, and cassoulet of shellfish; treacle tart is available at lunchtime; in the evening Cointreau soufflé with orange and chocolate sauce. A vegetarian dish is available. The downstairs grill is a simpler, less formal restaurant, where roasts, grills, flambéd desserts and old favourites like trifle and bread-and-butter pudding are always available.

The eleven bedrooms in the main house give the delightful feeling of going back into a past setting without losing out on such amenities as television, radio, phone, plumbing and warmth. The decorative style of the bathrooms is Edwardian, but the bedrooms have been made eighteenth-century, with appropriate paintings, porcelain, plants and fabrics carefully chosen by Janey Compton of Newby Hall. One room has a *trompe l'œil* 'window view' of York racecourse on the wall. A more cottagey but equally comfortable ambience is provided by the conversion of the eighteenth-century redbrick stable block. Here there are individual rooms and suites as well as a separate cottage. A restored late seventeenth-century dovecot near the restored gardens has become a wine store, where tastings are occasionally held.

Although Riber Hall dates from the 1400s, it calls itself 'an Elizabethan country house hotel', the last building additions having been made in 1661. Surrounded by small market towns, it is not far south of Sheffield near the Derbyshire peak district and within easy reach of houses like Chatsworth, Haddon Hall and Hardwick Hall, the last famously 'more glass than wall'. But it is one of those tucked-away spots that makes one reluctant to venture far from the grounds. The gardens, though not large, are like separate walled and lawned 'rooms', opening off one another in terraces. Even on a wet day their plants can be enjoyed from a garden room area with sofa and magazines, surrounded by greenery. The entrance, with its tiny reception area, is a flagged corridor roofed with glass and hung with vines and plants.

The public rooms have a heavier period feel, with stone doorways and tall Jacobean-style chairs. The drawing room is also furnished in heavy Jacobean style, the whole house having been renovated in the 1970s from a more or less derelict state. The sitting room has a beamed ceiling, little oak tables, velvet sofas, and an elaborately carved fireplace.

In the dining room, which has a lighter atmosphere, a central heavy oak table acts as a buffet, surrounded by polished tables set with candles and flowers. Lunch and dinner are both served. Salmon mousse tart with chive cream, and smoked fish platter with sour cream dressing are highlights of the menu, which includes good fish, game and roast meats as well as traditional country puddings. There is also a vegetarian menu.

The eleven bedrooms are all across a courtyard in the old stable block. Pleasantly quiet, they are set in half-timbered walls, with whitewashed walls, exposed stonework and leaded windows. They all have views of the garden, and one room (No. 10) has steps leading down to it. The period atmosphere is underlined by one of the best hotel collections of four-posters (nine rooms have them, and the one half-tester is older still). The beds show how each can become an individually furnished 'room'. One is of solid carved oak with a wooden top, crimson gold-edged drapes and a cover embroidered for the Queen's Jubilee in 1977. A second has finely carved posts, and top and back hung with floral fabric. A feminine version has a pink padded headboard and pink linings to the floral-patterned cover and valence.

Riber Hall
Matlock, Derbyshire
DE4 5JU
☎ (0629) 582795
Owners: Alex and Gill Biggin.
Member of Pride of Britain
Price grid B

Location: Leave the M1 at Exit 28 and take the A38 to Alfreton, and then the A615 towards Matlock; at Tansley (before Matlock) turn left to Riber and Riber Hall. 20 minutes from M1.

Riber Hall has one of the best collections of four-poster beds.

SCOTLAND

Monarchs of the Glens

Society's summer route to recovery from the exigencies of the London Season is traditionally by way of Scotland. In August Scotland is the place to be, as house parties gather for salmon fishing and the Glorious Twelfth. Once mothers whose debutante daughters had not made the engagement stakes by the time Henley was well over used to take them north of the border in the hope that they would mate up with a likely laird, and elaborate dances were held on the Isle of Skye and elsewhere.

It was Queen Victoria who put the royal stamp of approval on Scotland, discovering the delights of the Scottish summer over a century ago, and her annual and much enjoyed visits to Royal Deeside set a pattern that is faithfully followed by her descendants today with their long break at Balmoral and visits to the Highland games.

Scotland's often bloody and brutal history has acquired a veneer of romance for the visitor following in the tracks of Mary Queen of Scots and Bonnie Prince Charlie, of writers like Burns and Scott. Craggy castles are redolent of warring days and the need to defend and protect one's home and clansmen. Some of these have now let down their drawbridges to receive visitors. But many of the so-called castles were built or remodelled by wealthy English industrialists, who followed Victoria north for their holidays. They were very partial to castellated and turreted architecture, preferably in the puce red stone of Arran, which they moved about like the builders of the pyramids while paying the labourers a pittance. As one wit remarked of London's St Pancras station, they were defending themselves against the light artillery of the thirteenth century. An example of such a house, filled with international bric-à-brac brought back from world tours in the family steam yacht, is Kinloch Castle on the island of Rhum. Here the Bulloughs, the family of a Lancashire cotton machinery magnate, built an Edwardian retreat which is now maintained as a museum. All is just as they left it in 1914, and visitors can also stay overnight, eat off family silver and porcelain, and sleep under family portraits in bedrooms unaltered for over seventy years. Day visitors can peer at Sir George's figure-of-eight bath with wave-maker and sitz spray. Sir John Betjeman described the house as 'the stone embodiment of good King Edward's reign'. It has a piper's tower, a piper's covered colonnade walk, and double glazing (it helped against the gales). There used to be parrots and turtles in the grounds, where bananas were successfully grown in the west coast's milder climate. Meanwhile 44 indoor

Previous pages: Ardanaiseig overlooks Loch Awe.

servants looked after the family of sixteen and their guests.

Those heady house party days are largely gone, except in the country house hotels, but more and more of the many hunting and shooting lodges and grand holiday homes in Scotland are being turned into hotels of a high standard. Many have the plus of big estate grounds around them for sports. Cromlix is a classic example, in its five thousand acres, and is also one of those that stay open all year.

Having the space also makes it possible to provide helicopter landing facilities. Such is the affluence of some businesses that companies will fly top clients to Scotland and ferry them on by helicopter from the airport to a country house hotel and back again; so it is possible to leave London in the morning, lunch in the Highlands, perhaps have a round of golf, and get back in time for cocktails.

Greywalls does not fit the pseudo-baronial shooting house image. Its owner once described it succinctly as 'a small, albeit dignified, holiday home'. It does have grey walls; the house curved to the formal drive and opening out to the sheltered walled gardens behind. It was built in 1901 and, like Little Thakeham (page 44), it was designed by the collaboration of Sir Edwin Lutyens and Gertrude Jekyll. The original owner, the Hon. Alfred Lyttleton, had wanted turrets and large windows, but Lutyens said this was impossible. Greywalls is set where it is because Lyttleton was a keen golfer and wanted to be as close to the eighteenth hole of Muirfield as possible. The house is so close that golfers who stay in

Greywalls was called by Lutyens 'my favourite house'.

Greywall's garden gate in the gardens which were designed by Gertrude Jekyll.

the newer rooms added in 1972 can leave their rooms and walk across a small private patio garden right on to the course without being watched by anyone. Inevitably golfers are attracted to Greywalls, and the entrance lobby is covered with golfing prints, cartoons and souvenir memorabilia. Other attractions are the big sweeping dune beaches and the proximity to Edinburgh, while gardeners come to see Miss Jekyll's creation, which is largely as she designed it. The walled gardens, with their pleasant vistas of rose, creeper and orchard, are calm sun-traps, sheltered from the wind and perfect for drinks or lunch outside.

In 1908 the second owner, William James, commissioned Sir Robert Lorimer, the leading Scottish architect, to build on gate lodges and the 'nursery' wing on the west side. James's wife was a friend of King Edward, who stayed at Greywalls. The King liked to play cards in what is now the bar, and in the garden area where he exercised there is a changing room, now staff accommodation, known still as the 'king's loo'.

In 1924 the house was bought by Sir James Horlick as a holiday home. (He also owned the island of Gigha on the west coast of Scotland, which he enriched with a collection of rare plants in the Achamore Gardens). His daughter inherited Greywalls after its wartime service as a hospital for Polish forces and then as a maternity hospital. The Weavers wondered how to manage the upkeep of the house, and in 1948 made what was then the very brave decision to open the house as a hotel. It was difficult, to say the least, at a time of rationing. Coupons were allowed for the purchase of one set of sheets for guests, but none for the staff. Since then the main development has been the addition, in 1972, of a new dining room, bathrooms for all rooms, and five new bedrooms. The additions have been done in Lutyens character using Rattlebags stone, from a local quarry worked by monks, and tiles specially made in Holland. Lutyens stayed with Horlick at Greywalls and commented on the front lawn's flower-beds: 'What are those flower-beds doing drawing the eye off the beautiful lines of my favourite house?' They have been grassed over ever since.

The house is light and warm with corridors leading from the entrance to the sitting room and the cosy panelled library, which have open fires, paintings, plants and garden views. In the grounds are a tennis court and a croquet lawn, and there are ten golf courses within five miles. The Weavers recall a golfing guest who insisted his bed be lined up exactly north/south because the magnetic flow improved his game. The

Greywalls Hotel
Muirfield, Gullane, East Lothian EH31 2EG
☎ (0620) 842144
Owners: Mr and Mrs Giles Weaver
Manager: Henrietta Ferguson. Member of Pride of Britain
Price grid B
Notes: Closed end October to mid April (but house parties and small conferences accepted out of season)

Location: Take the A198 from Edinburgh towards North Berwick; Gullane is about 19 miles from Edinburgh, and Greywalls is signed on the approach to the village and is set at the east end of it, overlooking Muirfield golf course. By rail, to Edinburgh and local train to North Berwick (4½ miles).

bedrooms are furnished in Edwardian style, which has attracted romantic novelists to stay, most recently Barbara Cartland.

The dining room, once a courtyard, looks out on to the golf course and serves warming food to combat the fierce hunger brought on by sea air. Chef Robert Hood used to work at the Caledonian in Edinburgh. He presents a daily market menu: oak-smoked salmon comes with Greywalls garden salad on a 'moat' of fennel cream sauce with toasted honey brioche; local lobster is lightly sautéed with a little garlic and served on crisp salad with smoked lobster dressing; Aberdeen Angus beef comes with rich red wine and shallot sauce. The wine list is enlivened with reproductions of naughty rhymes and cartoons about wine.

The name Barjarg has medieval Gaelic origins, and means 'red hilltop fort'. Barjarg Tower is more the movie image of Scotland: Certainly a solid, turreted building with sheer walls, high windows and a lofty position on a hill, backed by thick woods. It is set in the Nith valley, and reached up a long curving drive that in spring is a river of daffodils. The Donaldson family, who moved here from the south, nursed the injured house back to life and health, although there is still work to be done on some of the towers. They bemoan the fact that few people know this quiet corner of Scotland and tear past on the A76, heading north or south. It is an area of rolling country-side, of rich agricultural land and wooded country. The house looks out along the Nith valley and offers private fishing on the Nith and shooting in season on local estates. A network of footpaths and forest trails is ideal for walkers. Dumfries is 11 miles away, the home of Robert Burns and a pleasant market town.

The house dates from 1580, but has Geor-gian and Edwardian additions. The oldest part houses a guest room, morning room and cellar. This was built by the Earl of Morton who was later Regent of Scotland when Mary Queen of Scots was imprisoned and was eventually executed for his part in the murder of Mary's

Barjarg Tower
Auldgirth, Dumfriesshire
DG2 0TN
☎ (0848) 31545
Owners: Archie and Mary Donaldson
Price grid C
Notes: Not suitable for young children. Kennels available in the grounds, but dogs not allowed in the house because of house pets.

Location: Travelling north on the A76 Dumfries/ Kilmarnock road, turn left about 8 miles north of Dumfries on to the road signed to Dunscore and Penpont; half a mile up the hill turn right for Penpont and Keir, and continue over the brow of the hill; the entrance gates are on the left about 1½ miles beyond the summit.
By rail, fast trains from London to Dumfries.

Barjarg tower the 'red hill top fort' is an imposing, sturdy house at the end of its long rising drive.

husband Darnley. The Hunter Arundells owned the house for over 250 years, and still own and farm the surrounding land. Barjarg once had an important library, housed in what is now the ballroom. It was used by Thomas Carlyle, the writer.

Archie Donaldson took early retirement in order to tackle the restoration, and with his family has worked to repulse the damp, repair the roof, make eight new bathrooms and put in 28 fire doors. James Noble was asked to take care of the interior decoration. He used miles of fabric in what could have been a dour setting. Comfortable chairs, sofas and antiques with modern TV and telephone touches make colourful havens within the grey towers. The huge bay-windowed bedroom in the sixteenth-century tower has a king-sized bed in green and pink chintz and dressing-table skirts to match. Down a few steps is a separate bathroom, big and white. All the rooms are different shapes and have dramatic Noble bed backings, toning velvet sofas, and rich use of fabric throughout.

Mary runs the household side and fusses over the quality of the bathroom towels and the choice of toiletries and curtain colours. Archie supervises the cellar, with its vintage clarets and simpler table wines, and acts as wine waiter at dinner. At first they employed a butler, but found this too formal. Now they join guests for drinks in the drawing room, with its moulded ceiling, big fire, pale sofas, deep chairs and brocaded wall panels. This is a good opportunity to discuss the menu and ideas for sightseeing before moving into the panelled dining room. Here one can admire the superb work of a Belgian wood carver, who made the coats of arms over the fireplace, said to be a copy of one in Holyrood House. A five-course dinner menu, which changes daily, is prepared by a young Scots chef, Anne McCann, who has an imaginative line in soups; from cream of fennel to cream of red pepper and tomato. The entrée may be seafood pie, pâtés, Stilton eggs or smoked salmon; and main courses are based on traditional meat, fish and game from the locality. Puddings can include rhubarb pie, orange Pavlova, bread-and-butter pudding, walnut fudge tart or Ecclefechan tart, which is a cold tart of dried fruit, walnut and brown sugar served with cream. Lanark blue, the local ewe's milk cheese, and hand-made oat cakes round off the meal.

There is an in-house secretarial service, and business facilities are provided; but most guests are content to wander the 42 acres, seeing snow drops, daffodils and rhododendrons in seasonal bloom. The Donaldsons say their next big task is to create a woodland garden.

Cromlix is the warmest of all country house hotels and offers a wide range of sporting activities on its 5000-acre estate.

The long Cromlix drive is a fitting prelude to the 5,000-acre estate in which this Edwardian shooting lodge is set. The visitor is surprised at the instant welcome from staff the moment he parks (they have a television 'eye' in the office). Whatever the weather outside, all year round Cromlix belies the theory that country houses are cold. Ronald Eden likes his house well heated, and there is central heating, as well as open fires, electric blankets (switched on each evening unless the guests request not) and gas 'log' fires in the rooms to keep everyone snug.

Outside, the 1880 house once visited by Edward VII, is undistinguished creeper clad with a bulge showing the location of the chapel. A flock of Jacob sheep graze alongside the house; their wool is knitted into a range of goods for sale, among the most appealing being the 'portrait' sweater of Domino, the master ram of the flock.

Cromlix has been in the Eden family for four hundred years and contains many family possessions. Ronald Eden's mother embroidered the hangings in the chapel, and one can enjoy Bateman cartoons in the bathrooms, peer at military ancestors at famous battles in prints on the toilet walls, and read copies of *Punch* and *Country Life* set out on the broad wooden thunderbox seats – so comfortable and efficient a piece of plumbing – in some of the rooms.

Cromlix arranges shooting breaks and fishing holidays on their private lochs, while golf can be played at Gleneagles, or the Jackie Stewart shooting school and Mark Phillips equestrian centre sampled there. Even the

Cromlix House
Kinbuck, Dunblane,
Perthshire FK15 9JJ
☎ (0786) 822125
Owner: The Hon. Ronald Eden
General Manager: Grant Howlett. Member of Pride of Britain
Price grid A
Notes: Dogs welcomed

Location: Take the M9 and A9 from Edinburgh towards Perth; at Dunblane take the B8033 towards Kinbuck and ¼ mile north over a hump-backed bridge, Cromlix House signed on left.

worst weather can be enjoyed in leisured comfort indoors at Cromlix. I have always yearned to have the time to spend hours curled up on the highly cushioned day bed built into the turret area of the Upper Turret suite, my favourite, and read all day – perhaps Eden's book on shooting. Eight of the fourteen rooms are suites. The Upper Turret, for example, has a long pink-lined corridor from a little lobby with rooms leading off; a sitting room with dining table (for room service and butler service for dinner in the suites can be arranged at an extra charge), a dressing room/bathroom and a bed-room.

A balustraded staircase hung with portraits sweeps down to the inner hall which is warmed by a log fire and leads to the morning room, with its marble fireplace, chintzy yellow chairs, big bay windows, papers and books. It has the perfect country house hotel 'bar': bottles are piled in an antique invalid chair. There is also a library for quiet retreats.

In fine weather, guests like to walk, or order a picnic hamper – a proper one with rugs, crystal and china – and take it perhaps by family pony trap or 1930s Rolls-Royce, to a private lochside. Tennis and riding on the estate and croquet on the back lawn can also be sampled.

The dining room, as befits the setting, is small and has a house party atmosphere. Plenty of game is served, recreating the Eden family collection of game recipes. In autumn the house lays on special festivals of game recipes. Chef Mark Salter, who has worked at Baden Baden's Brenners Park, cooks the whole range of wild meats and fish with herb and berry accompani-ments, and his fruity desserts cleanse the palate. Breakfasts are bracing Edwardian affairs: the choice includes kippers, smoked haddock and egg with black pudding. Cromlix is starting to smoke its own produce and supply game items by mail order; it will also be running more themed food and wine weekends, includ-ing tea and potato tastings.

The house was built in 1832 to a design by William Burn with crow-stepped gable in Scottish Jacobean style. In 1887 the south wing and terraces were added and the interior was remodelled in ornate Renaissance style. The owner, James Reid, derived his riches from building locomotives in Glasgow at a time when rich Glaswegians built country residences within fairly easy reach of the city. Reid's art collection was given to the Glasgow art gallery after his death. The wealth to be gained then from supplying locomotives to the railways of the world is seen the moment one enters the house. The marble entrance has a

Auchterarder House
Auchterarder, Perthshire
PH3 1DL
☎ (07646) 2939/3646/7
Owners: Ian and Audrey Brown. Member of Prestige
Price grid A

Location: Take the A9 north from Edinburgh and go through Dunblane; at Auchterarder turn left on to B8062 road to Crieff; Auchterarder House is not far along this road on right. Helicopter pad.

heavy wooden ceiling, leather wallpaper on the upper walls, inlaid tiling and carving over weighty doors; and the sumptuous wood panelling continues along the main hall and around the fireplace and leather sofas of the front hall. The main staircase is balustraded and overlooked by stags' heads. The library is filled with leather chairs, and its marble fireplace is upheld by busts of Homer and Plato. Panelled oak doors connect to the drawing room, with its chandeliers and mirrored overmantel. The dining room also has solid wood doors and a tiled fireplace.

The conservatory, all marble and mosaics, leading to the old billiards room is another ostentatious period piece, with its marble pillared entrance, 1890 terrazzo floor and central fountain. It is a now a lovely plant-hung setting for dinner parties. The old billiards room has a massive fireplace, hung with portraits, a high beamed ceiling, family shields as decoration and double doors at one end leading to the croquet lawn. It now also has a small bar.

Guests must ring for admittance, but this, as a note by the doorbell states, is 'not to exclude but to welcome to our house'. The Brown family say they run Auchterarder as a house with a hotel licence. They have kept the house as far as possible in its authentic period form, even the spacious bedrooms. The Graham and Gordon rooms have fine examples of 1901 built-in mahogany furniture, and the Stuart room has its original Victorian bathroom with a glazed and brass-edged shower stall at one end of the bath, its claw feet delicately screened with a velvet pelmet. There is also an oval dressing mirror and basin set in a brass stand.

Auchterarder House was built in splendour by a Victorian locomotive manufacturer.

Detailing is of top quality, with velvet button-back chairs, crystal glasses in the bedrooms, lamps, drapes and wallpapers all in Victorian style. A decanter of sherry and flowers provide a welcome in the rooms. The bathrooms are equipped with separate shower cubicle, bidet, vanity unit, heated towel rail and hair-drier. There is a 24-hour room service. 'Cunningham', the old morning room downstairs, is a big, light bedroom suitable for the disabled.

Meal charges include house cocktail, canapés, coffee and *petits fours*. The dining room tables are set with individual silver napkin rings among the finery. The Browns' son Paul is chef and has an 'auld alliance' mix of French and Scottish ideas. One of his menus might include a French snail casserole; a warm salad with *foie gras* and truffles; a roulade of fresh Scottish salmon, rainbow trout and herring in white wine, orange and herb marinade; a chilled peppered avocado and nut terrine; and venison Balmoral flambéed in port with a sweet and sour cranberry sauce. A dessert speciality named after James Reid consists of pears poached in a rich punch, stuffed with apple and pear mousseline and spiked with fresh ginger on a Chantilly of Seville orange.

The 17½-acre grounds are filled with over four hundred species of trees and plants which Reid brought back from his locomotive-selling trips all over the world. They include splendid Wellingtonias, and there is a fern leaf beech which is older than the house. Golf can be arranged at Gleneagles, two miles away, and fishing and shooting are available. Private shooting parties can be arranged on a 4,000-acre estate nearby.

Invery is one of the prettiest of country house hotels. It certainly is not heavy or baronial and leaves an impression of lightness, flowers and charm. The approach is a narrow lane which twists through high trees and past mossy banks filled with wild flowers by the little River Feugh. It was built in 1795 and later Sir Walter Scott was a regular visitor and wrote many poems at Invery including 'Marmion', and the Spences have named the rooms after the titles of Scott novels.

The Spences recently spent 1½ years in restoring the house from an empty shell. For them it was the fulfilment of a dream; they were previously hotel owners in Aberdeen. They have also restored the gardens, sheltered by old walls and wide flower-beds. Organic tunnels will provide fruit and vegetables for the hotel. The entrance is circular before a long reception salon with a wooden floor where the Spences plan to hold entertainments. The drawing room

Invery House
Banchory, Royal Deeside, Kincardineshire AB3 0NJ
☎ (03302) 4782
Owners: Stewart and Sheila Spence
General Manager: Tom Ward. Member of Prestige
Price grid A
Notes: No children under 8 years. Free kennels in grounds for dogs; no dogs allowed in the house

Location: Take the A93 from Aberdeen along Deeside to Banchory; in town turn left on to the B974, which wriggles along by the Bridge of Feugh; Invery House is signed on the right.

fireplace has a coal fire; and there is an octagonal room off the dining room where Scott is said to have written part of 'Marmion'.

Keen fishermen are regular guests at Invery House.

The fourteen bedrooms are showcases for fabrics and antiques. There are brass bedsteads with crown canopies, four posters hung in turquoise and pink with a pink sofa at the foot, high carved Continental beds with matching mirrored wardrobe. Alcoves under the eaves have been cleverly utilised in one room to form a tent of blue pleated fabric over the bed. There is satellite television and phones in the bathrooms. Even the ladies' loo in the old billiards room has floral painted toilets and basins. The fishing guests who come to angle in the Dee somehow look a little too hearty against the ubiquitous delicate floral background.

The dining room contains big padded armchairs in which you can peruse Kenneth McPhee's menus. McPhee, who used to be at Inverlochy Castle (see page 184) gets his smoked salmon from an Aberdeen firm and plenty of fish from the market. Stewart Spence believes in Scottish food with its French traditions and here you could find a starter of smoked quail and venison salad with croutons and Cumberland sauce, or curried turnip soup with toasted almonds; a main course of roast chicken with buckwheat stuffing, or fillets of trout with spring onions and ginger in a spiced cream sauce; and for dessert an apple-filled *crêpe* with brown sugar and cream.

There is salmon and sea trout fishing on the Feugh, which runs for a mile through the Invery grounds, and the hotel also has boats on the River Dee. There are grouse and pheasant moors, as well as several golf clubs nearby.

Tullich Lodge proudly flies the flag on Royal Deeside.

Like John Tovey, Francis Coulson and Brian Sack in the Lakes, Neil Bannister and Hector Macdonald have pioneered the idea of a personalized country house setting and a set menu with good-quality food. Like other pioneers they were not fully appreciated at first, but Tullich is a comfortable, lived-in place where gossip and good after dinner conversation reigns and the guest is cared for like a person rather than just a customer.

Hector Macdonald, who runs the front of house, was an Edinburgh printer, and Neil Bannister trained as a chef with Grand Metropolitan. They serve high tea to children in the kitchen which, together with the adjacent office, becomes the hub of the house. Another popular place is the first-floor sitting room, with its piles of books, papers and magazines; this is a good place to sit and talk or take a buttery (Aberdeen's answer to the croissant) with black coffee after indulging too long and late on Lochnagar, the local malt whisky. The tall, narrow, turreted stone house looks out to the Coyles of Muick and the dark hump of Lochnagar, immortalized by Byron and the Prince of Wales, which was once a volcano and is now a deep loch.

Tullich does also have a bar, but it's more like a mini pub or club, not in the least haughty or formal. It has old bottles for decoration, toy trains run around the walls, and there is a small peat fire. Hector serves guests and often members of the Balmoral household come down for a drink; then Hector and Neil have to talk in code when referring to the royals, so that guests aren't aware.

Tullich Lodge
By Ballater, Aberdeenshire
AB3 5SB
☎ (0338) 55406
Owners: Neil Bannister and Hector Macdonald. Member of Pride of Britain
Price grid A (includes dinner)
Notes: Closed November to April. Dogs welcome but not in the public rooms.

Location: Take the A93 Aberdeen to Braemar road; Tullich is signed to the right 1 mile before Ballater, and approached by a short steep drive.

Ballater's quiet prosperity grew up after it became the rail head for Queen Victoria's visits to Balmoral. Tullich village, of which little remains, was once the oldest Royal Burgh on Deeside, first settled at the time of the Picts. In 1897 an Aberdeen advocate built Tullich Lodge on a wooded knoll overlooking the river. Today delightful natural wooded gardens spill down the hill, with shrubs and flowers framing the lawns and the views of the valley. Tullich is built in local pink granite with a baronial turret, crenellations and crow steps; a Scottish flag flies from the roof. The bedrooms are neat, and those on the upper two floors all have a private bathroom (two have a shower room); for those who don't mind the extra climb there is also the Tower room on the third floor.

Tullich's aim is to relax their guests, and bookings for large functions are rarely accepted. The dining room has original mahogany panelling with bird's-eye effects. Polished tables reflect silver and crisp linen. With notice, diet and vegetarian meals can be prepared. Otherwise the set menu may include items like pike dumplings with mushroom and cheese sauce; roast loin of venison with rowan jelly; baked lemon sole with crab and seaweed and white wine sauce; poached pheasant egg with watercress mayonnaise; and puddings such as gooseberry and orange pie with almond crust, old-fashioned Bakewell tart, Bramley apple pie, Eve's pudding and bramble ice cream.

Culloden House is said to have been used as battle headquarters by Bonnie Prince Charlie.

Culloden House has glamorous associations with the Rebellion of 1745, when Bonnie Prince Charlie attempted to regain the British throne for the Stuarts, and almost succeeded, but met his final, crushing defeat at the battle of Culloden in 1746. The owner of the house then was Duncan Forbes, who deprived the prince of the support of ten thousand men. Nevertheless, when the prince captured the house and used it as his battle headquarters he refused to let his men despoil it. After the battle the victorious Duke of Cumberland took up residence found wounded Jacobite officers there and had them shot in the dungeon where the hotel now has its sauna.

Given this historical build-up, the surrounding modern village is a disappointing eyesore which detracts from the beauty of the classic façade, with its sweep of lawns, edged with trees, in its forty acres of grounds. Inside the house the bedroom decor is patchy, a jumble of indifferent furniture and uncoordinated fabrics. Best are the newly decorated attic rooms, which have more of a country house feel than the larger of the first-floor rooms, one of which was used by Prince Charles (the current one)

Culloden House
Inverness, Inverness-shire
IV1 2NZ
☎ (0463) 790461
Owners: Ian and Marjory McKenzie. Member of Prestige
Price grid A

Location: Take the A96 from Inverness towards Nairn; 3 miles from centre of Inverness take right turn to Culloden; the hotel is 1 mile on, on the left-hand side. By air to Inverness Dalcross airport (6 miles). By rail Inverness station is 15 miles away. Helicopter pad.

on a formal visit.

The McKenzies make the most of the historical setting, even running special battle anniversary weekends. They love the house, and live in a converted dungeon with their collie dogs. They wear the kilt for dinner, and on the lawn on summer evenings a piper plays. The public rooms are a good background for historical evocation, especially the Adam-style plaster work and chintz sofas under the chandeliers in the drawing room at the back of the house. Opening off it is the Adam dining room, with dark green walls and raised white medallions recalling Wedgwood sage Jasper ware. Michael Simpson the chef, who trained at Gleneagles and has worked in Germany, creates Scottish fare with French presentation ideas. Starters may include game terrine with Cumberland sauce (an unfortunate name in this house), followed by medallions of marinated venison loin topped with apples and blackcurrants in a port wine sauce, sliced beef fillet with fresh *foie gras* filling and creamed spinach, and breast of chicken and crab meat deep fried in breadcrumbs.

Hand-carved animals and plants on the staircase at Arisaig.

Getting to Arisaig makes it seem more cut off from the world than it actually is; it certainly must have seemed remote to Bonnie Prince Charlie, fleeing from the battlefield of Culloden. After Fort William the 'road to the isles' winds alongside lochs, past stone cottages, below lowering hills, often narrowing to a single track with passing places.

Down off the road, sheltered by tall trees and hills to the east, Arisaig is a grey and Gothic-looking house with a big entrance courtyard. Its little towers were built in 1864 to designs by Philip Webb and are now listed as of architectural interest. To the south there are views of the loch and sound of Arisaig, which can be reached through beautifully kept terraced gardens, with woodland walks and flowering shrubs, and then through sheep pasture to rocky finger inlets. Following the walks outlined in a leaflet, one can clamber up among thin trees to find Bonnie Prince Charlie's cave, a tiny cavern enclosed by rock, that would indeed be virtually impossible to find, but a dank and constricting place in which to hide.

The house is relaxing, so much so that guests have been known to cry when the time has come to leave. The sixteen bedrooms have been thoughtfully furnished by Ruth Smither, and her husband brings items back from his frequent journeys to London. The bedrooms, named after Scottish lochs, are reached by a staircase carved with plants and animals. Some of the rooms have window seats from which to enjoy the loch and hill views. For four years the

Arisaig House
Beasdale, Arisaig,
Inverness-shire PH39 4NR
☎ (06875) 622
Owners: John and Ruth
Smither. Member of Relais
et Châteaux
Manager: son-in-law David
Williiams
Price grid A (includes dinner)
Notes: Closed November to
Easter. No children under 10
years; no dogs.

Location: From Fort William
take the A830 road towards
Mallaig; Arisaig House is on
this road before the village of
Arisaig, and one mile from
Beasdale station. By rail
from London Euston to
Mallaig, alighting at Beasdale
station (overnight sleepers
available). Helicopter Pad.

*Adam-style plaster work in
Culloden House dining room.*

Smithers had looked all over the UK for a country house to turn into a hotel, before falling in love with empty Arisaig and its sunset views. In the Second World War, the house was the Special Operations headquarters where Odette Churchill, among others, was trained to be dropped behind enemy lines.

The food served relies a lot on garden produce. Local produce frequently accompanies sophisticated additions, so that squat lobster comes with samphire (an asparagus-like marsh plant), *foie gras* with rowan jelly, mussels with saffron cream, and smoked shellfish with watercress and avocado mousse. But most ingredients are left fairly plain to let the flavour come through.

Inverlochy Castle inspired Queen Victoria to write 'I never saw a lovelier or more romantic spot'.

Inverlochy has long been established as one of the finest hotels in Britain. It was set up in 1969 by Grete Hobbs after the death of her husband, who had bought the property in 1944, and she has run it ever since. The nineteenth-century house is a castle only in the Victorian baronial sense. Solid and turreted, it is set smugly in woods below the smooth rises of the Ben Nevis range and overlooks its 'house' loch and its own 500-acre grounds. The house was built by Lord Abinger in 1870 for his American bride, near the site of a thirteenth-century fortress. Queen Victoria spent a week at Inverlochy in 1873 and wrote enthusiastically in her diary, 'I never saw a lovelier or more romantic spot.'

The romance of the wild sweeps of scenery has its counterpart in the ornate richness of the interiors. The entrance hall has a finely painted ceiling with a central oval of cherubs gambolling in a blue sky, chandeliers and double windows. It feels like the heart of the house, with its big oriental rugs, portraits and oil paintings, and velvet chairs around the fireplace. A wooden staircase leads from here to the sixteen bedrooms, most of which have day beds, big windows, plenty of chintz, television (the house has two masts), paintings of Bonnie Prince Charlie and arched sitting areas; one has little purple glass chandeliers. The drawing room below is long and light, with several windows and a gold and pink colour scheme.

The dining room has a view over the loch from its bay window and the room is characterised by brocaded chairs, polished wood tables and a long carved sideboard set with silver and topped with life-size cockerels. Here Graham Newbold the chef (formerly at the Connaught restaurant and Buckingham and Kensington palaces) serves local produce and seafood in classical ways: cream and white onion soup with onion *confit*; cold Loch Linnhe

Inverlochy Castle
Torlundy, Fort William
PH33 6SN
☎ (0397) 2177
Owner: Mrs Grete Hobbs
Managing Director: Michael Leonard. Member of Relais et Châteaux
Price grid A
Notes: Closed mid November to second week of March. Children under 12 years only in parents' room. No dogs.

Location: Inverlochy is 3 miles north of Fort William on the A82, just past the golf club.
By rail to Fort William which also has a heliport.

prawns with fennel sauce, casserole of pigeon, walnut mousse with caramelized pear in almond pastry, hot rhubarb soufflé with lemon cream – all superbly presented and served by waitresses dressed in black and white.

Though only half an hour further south than Arisaig, Glenborrodale Castle seems more isolated. Getting there takes longer, and those who miss the last ferry at 9 p.m. have to drive a long way round through Fort William. The turn-of-the-century castle was built in a superbly sheltered spot, where its puce turrets peep from among the trees and the castle is only really visible from a boat coming in from Mull nearby. It was built by C. D. Rudd, a friend of Cecil Rhodes, who like Rhodes owned a share in the De Beer gold and diamond fields. The castle took three years to build, using red sandstone brought from the Isle of Arran, and was embellished with rare plants and trees, principally rhododendrons. A palm tree bears witness to the mildness of the climate; but dry it is not. This is one of the wetter parts of Britain, with an annual rainfall of six feet.

It was already a hotel when Peter de Savary bought it in 1987 and set about restoring the qualities of a country house. Before they became hotel managers here, Susan Carroll was a fitness instructor, and Charles a P and O purser. De Savary does not have a chef as such; girl cooks from a top London agency prepare the excellent meals. There is no room service, but guests can make tea and coffee in the rooms. Nor is there a bar, but Patrick, the young tree surgeon who doubles as hall porter, pours drinks in the old billiards room, with its dog pictures, deer heads, huge video and Victorian piano organ. The staff tend to be versatile here: Alison, the young beautician, doubles as receptionist and can unblock a drain if need be. The public rooms are dotted with framed photos of Peter de Savary and his family and he reserves the top room in one turret for his own visits.

In the grounds there are walled kitchen gardens, which are being built up to provide vegetables, herbs, fruit and flowers. There is also a lake, as well as croquet and tennis, and trails leading down to the beach. Here there is a boat-house where windsurfers are kept. Further round on the rocks, seals also come out to sun, and de Savary owns a couple of islands in the sound where guests can be ferried for day visits and picnics. The hotel has a few boats moored at its own anchorages which may also be used by visiting yachtsmen. Guests can hire boats for day trips, principally to Mull, Iona and

Glenborrodale Castle
Acharacle Ardnamurchan
Peninsula, Argyll PH36 4JP
☎ (097) 24 266
Proprietor: Peter de Savary
Managers: Charles and
Susan Carroll
Price grid A
Note: Closed end October till
Easter.

Location: Take the A82 from
Glasgow through Glencoe; at
Onich take the Corran ferry
(10 minutes) to Strontian;
continue to Salen on the
A861; turn left on to the
B8007 to Acharacle;
Glenborrodale Castle is on
the right past Borrodale
village.
By helicopter to
neighbouring farm land.

Glenborrodale Castle was built in the nineteenth century in red Arran sandstone.

Staffa. Tobermory, the 'capital' of Mull, is only thirty minutes away by boat. In July and August there are regattas and island races.

The castle has a 500-acre farm nearby, where there is space for off-road vehicle driving, a trout loch, and opportunities for clay pigeon shooting, riding and walking; there are 120 acres of grounds around the castle itself. Wellies and sports equipment are available.

The Victorian decorative theme has been sustained within the castle with lots of cushions, bric-à-brac, china and paintings. The stone spiral staircase leading to the rooms is hung with framed tartan designs. The bedrooms are named after famous Scotsmen. The bathrooms have an old-fashioned feel, some of them furnished with velvet chairs. The bedroom walls are hung with china and botanical prints, and rooms have Austrian window blinds and chinoiserie lamps; they all have sitting areas, and some have four-poster beds. There are stunning sea views from the windows.

Breakfast is taken in the panelled dining room, hung with heavy Victorian pictures and tapestries. Light lunches can be taken in a conservatory room by the lawn. Dinner is the more leisurely meal, and the menu may include such dishes as warm salmon mousse with watercress sauce, rack of lamb with orange and port sauce, shepherds pie, steak and kidney pie, and desserts like Queen of Puddings.

Approached along a road punctuated by cattle grids, Ardanaiseig is literally the end of the road; near Oban, yet more approachable by boat on Loch Awe. The surrounding gardens, a blur of bluebells, azaleas and rhododendrons in late spring, are open to the public and there are walks around the shrubs and blooms. Woodland and forestry trails are indicated, and there is fishing for salmon and brown trout in the estate's small hill loch, while beginners can angle for rainbow trout in a duck pond near the hotel.

The house was built by Colonel James Campbell, father of fifteen children, in 1834. On Sunday mornings the colonel would select from his many daughters those who should row him across the loch to church. A teetotaller, a non-smoker, churchman and also very rich, Campbell required his guests to bring their own liquor, consume it in private and clean up any evidence. He also had liberal political views and helped found the forerunner of the National Farmers Union. In 1880 a Cumbrian industrialist bought the property and changed the name to Ardainaiseig, meaning 'the point by the ferry'. The present owners bought the house from the man who wrote the song 'The Man who Broke the Bank at Monte Carlo'; they have restored the gardens and have opened them to the public to raise money for charity.

The architect was William Burn, one of the four architects who, after the death of Robert Adam, executed his plans for the New Town of Edinburgh (see also Auchterarder House). Burn also designed Bowhill for the Duke of Buccleugh, and the listed exterior of Ardanaiseig is virtually unchanged. In former days the house flew a flag when it wanted the Loch Awe steamer to stop at the house. After a gap of fifty years the steamer service has just been reintroduced, using a 36-foot steam launch that carries thirty passengers and was built on Lake Windermere in 1926.

Rare specimen trees surround the house and when the house was first being built, oak trees larger than any previously known were found. Near the entrance to the garden are two groves of Canadian maples planted to commemorate the centenary of the Confederacy of Canada. The hotel has its own pier on Loch Awe and boats for fishing, exploring and picnicking on the many islands. More serious fishermen have access to a boat on a river, and there are hill lochs nearby; clay pigeon shooting is also available.

Ardanaiseig's bedrooms are large and chintzy with lots of flowers on polished tables. There is a 1930s feel about the furnishings. The recently redecorated dining room offers food created by young Scottish chefs. Currently Lindsay Little prepares a daily five-course dinner menu which is included in the room price. This may start with carrot consommé or smoked venison salad; there is always a fresh fish dish such as scallops with filo pastry and caviar, followed by the main meat course, a choice of puddings, and the cheeseboard with apples and celery.

Ardanaiseig
Kilchrenan, by Tainuilt, Argyll
☎ (08663) 333
Owners: Jonathan and Jane Brown. Member Pride of Britain
Price grid A (includes dinner)
Notes: Closed late October till mid-April. No children under 8 years. Dogs by arrangement when booking.

Location: Take the A85 Perth to Oban road; at Taynuilt take the B845 to Kilchrenan; go through village and follow the side of Loch Awe to Ardanaiseig at the end of the road.
By rail to Oban via Crianlarich. Helicopter pad.

A detail from the fireplace at Ardanaiseig.

ELGIN

INVERNESS
96

ABERDEEN
95 94

North Sea

97

99 98

DUNDEE

PERTH
92 93
100

EDINBURGH 90

GLASGOW
BERWICK

STRANRAER

DUMFRIES 91

82

NEWCASTLE

CARLISLE 81 DURHAM
79 80
76
77 78
74 75
73 83 84
85
LANCASTER 86 87 YORK
88
BRADFORD LEEDS

LIVERPOOL
MANCHESTER

SHEFFIELD LINCOLN

CHESTER
68 89
69 70 72 71
STOKE ON TRENT
67 NOTTINGHAM
DERBY GRANTHAM 57
55 KINGS LYNN
SHREWSBURY 53 56 NORWICH
66 BURTON ON TRENT 54
LEICESTER
51
BIRMINGHAM
61 52 WARWICK CAMBRIDGE
WORCESTER 42 IPSWICH
65 43 STRATFORD ON AVON BEDFORD 59 58
64 41 7 60
HEREFORD 62 48 49
MONMOUTH 44 6
45 50 OXFORD 10
47 9 ST. ALBANS
SWANSEA
CARDIFF HENLEY 1 LONDON
63 BRISTOL 2 8
34 46 32 3 CANTERBURY 15
35 31 BATH 21 12 DOVER
33 36 4 5 11
37 30 22 13 17
GLASTONBURY WINCHESTER 16 18 14
38 SALISBURY 23
29 27 24 20 BRIGHTON
EXETER 28 26 25 19
39

PLYMOUTH 40

0   50 miles
0   50   100km

INDEX OF HOTELS

Map references are in bold numerals, page references are in italics

THE SEASON

A few essentials:

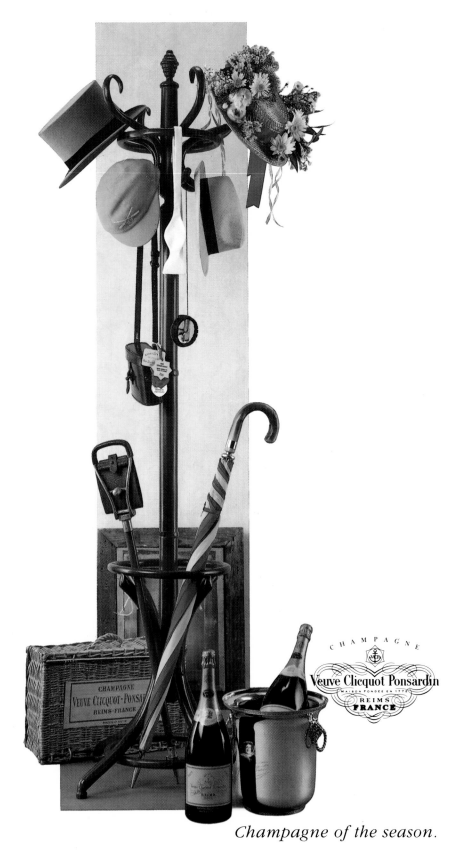

Champagne of the season.

ACKNOWLEDGEMENTS

I would like to thank the hoteliers who helped with information, time and guidance round their properties even when I dropped in without warning and at busy, inconvenient moments. I would especially like to thank the following who gave me much wise advice as well as generous hospitality; Martin Skan at Chewton Glen, Peter Herbert at Gravetye, John Tovey at Miller Howe, John and Ruth Smither at Arisaig House, David and Ruth Watson at Hintlesham Hall, Bob and Wendy Payton at Stapleford Park, Christopher Coles at Lucknam Park, Ronald Eden and Grant Howlett at Cromlix, Trevor and Christine Forecast at Congham Hall, Ian Brown at Auchterarder House, John Sinclair and Nicola Roberts at Cliveden, Emyr Griffiths of Welsh Rarebits who introduced me to Egerton Grey and its delightful hosts, Richard Broyd of Historic House Hotels for the preview of Hartwell and to Anne Copp for taking me there; Carah Samuel at Scott Gold Blyth Public Relations for helping with Pride of Britain contacts, Sandra Lawson and Jill Faulds at Prestige hotels for their assistance.

I wrote most of this book at my own scrap of country house life, a listed seventeenth century cottage. I worked partly in the bathroom, partly on the landing, a little in the spare room and finally in my ex-kitchen study while builders and thatchers restored and extended the house. So I appreciate a little of what country house hotel owners go through to recreate and maintain the private house historical fabric for all to enjoy. Finally, thanks to my editors at Pavilion, Vivien Bowler and Jillie Norrey, to Eric Crichton for his evocative photographs and to my husband, Michael Geare who helped with the chauffeuring.

USEFUL ADDRESSES

Many of the hotels in the book are members of various marketing organisations which will supply brochures and information and make bookings if required.

Prestige Hotels, 353 The Strand, London WC2P 0HS. (01 240 2200 or reservations 0800 282124). In New York: 152 Madison Avenue, New York 10016. (212 779 1888; free 800 5447570).

Relais et Châteaux; directories available from French Government Tourist Office, 178 Piccadilly, London W1 (01 493 3171). In New York, David Mitchell and Company, 200 Madison Avenue, New York 10016. (212 696 1323).

Pride of Britain hotels are represented by Abercrombie and Kent, Sloane Square House, Holbein Place, London SW1W 8NS. (01 730 9600). In the USA, Abercrombie and Kent, 1420 Kensington Road, Oak Brook, Illinois 60521/2106. (312 954 2944 and toll free 800 323 3602).

Wolsey Lodges, 17 Chapel Street, Bideston, Suffolk IP7 7EP. (0449 741297).

Welsh Rarebits, City Travel Ltd, 13 Duke Street, Cardiff CF1 2AY, Wales. (0222 395317).

Historical castles and country inns, grand hotels and exotic resorts are the inspiration for our creativity at WAT&G. We invite you to explore this rich and wonderful legacy.

Wimberly Allison Tong & Goo
Architects and Planners